Praise for
Sis, Don't Settle

"If there's one person we can count on for level-headed advice, it's Faith. She has proven that if you live authentically and listen to that inner voice, you can have a life that exceeds your expectations. A must read!"
—Sunny Hostin, *New York Times* bestselling author of *Summer on Sag Harbor*

"Judge Faith Jenkins is the personification of what it means to live by faith! I was honored to marry her and her husband, the legendary Kenny Lattimore, and I know firsthand that she is a testament to never settling for less especially when it comes to love. I have no doubt her story, her wisdom, and her insights will motivate every reader to never settle for less than their worth!"
—DeVon Franklin, *New York Times* bestselling author of *The Wait*

"This is the best book on how to handle and cope with the different levels you can experience in dating, relationships, and situationships! Faith is smart, wise, and she kept me laughing and inspired. She's the voice you need to cut through all the drama to get on a clear-cut path toward high-value love."
—Angela Rye, host of *On One with Angela Rye* podcast

"Faith is all about believing, and she takes the knowledge, wit, and discernment that we love about her in the courtroom and writes it into every page of *Sis, Don't Settle*. This book is a must read, and it's absolutely amazing!" —Tia Mowry, author of *The Quick Fix Kitchen*

"I was relieved that *Sis Don't Settle* is not about 'catching' a man. This easy, wise, and often funny read is about recognizing your innate worth. Read this book. Love yourself. Then, expect more love to enter your life."

—Tina Lifford, author of *The Little Book of Big Lies*

Sis, Don't Settle

Sis, Don't Settle

How to Stay Smart in Matters of the Heart

Faith Jenkins

LEGACY
LIT

NEW YORK

Copyright © 2021 by Faith Jenkins

Cover design by Sara Wood

Cover photograph © Barry Morgenstein

Cover copyright © 2023 by Hachette Book Group, Inc.

Legacy Lit, an imprint of Grand Central Publishing
Hachette Book Group
1290 Avenue of the Americas
New York, NY 10104

LegacyLitBooks.com

Twitter.com/LegacyLitBooks

Instagram.com/LegacyLitBooks

Originally published in hardcover and ebook by Legacy Lit in November 2021
First trade paperback edition: November 2023

Grand Central Publishing is a division of Hachette Book Group, Inc. The Grand
Central Publishing and Legacy Lit name and logo is a trademark of the
Hachette Book Group.

The Hachette Speakers Bureau provides a wide range of authors for speaking
events. To find out more, go to hachettespeakersbureau.com or email
HachetteSpeakers@hbgusa.com.

Legacy Lit books may be purchased in bulk for business, educational, or promotional
use. For information, please contact your local bookseller or the Hachette Book
Group Special Markets Department at special.markets@hbgusa.com.

The publisher is not responsible for websites (or their content) that are not owned
by the publisher.

Library of Congress Cataloging-in-Publication Data has been applied for.

ISBNs: 978-0-306-92534-4 (trade paperback), 978-0-306-92532-0 (ebook)

Printed in the United States of America

LSC-C

Printing 1, 2023

To the women who choose to believe in the highest, grandest vision of love, this book is for you.

To my husband, Kenny—waiting for you to show up in my life was the best thing I ever did.

Contents

Part III
WHEN CONFLICT COMES KNOCKING

Introduction

Our Pledge

Sis, I know what you're thinking, there are so many books geared toward women about what to do to land a man. The truth is we don't have to do much. And the people who write such books tend to be men. I appreciate the advice our men have to offer, but there's only so much they can understand about being women in relationships—about as much as they know about Aunt Flo or strapless bras.

Sis, Don't Settle is for women not interested in metamorphosing into fishermen trying to "catch" a man or holding a player captive in a short-lived relationship. In this book, we're going to dig deep. We're not looking into how to manipulate anyone into a committed relationship. It's about becoming a woman with such a fulfilled life that anyone you bring to the table is only adding to the equation. This book is our book. It's about being centered on loving and growing no matter what Idris Elba creation walks into your life. It's a road map on how to play it smart, and manifest a destiny that involves ending up with someone ready and available for authentic love—no settling required!

If you're single, divorced, dating, happily un-entangled, or married, love is the universal language, and I want you to master that language. If the problems in love are universal, so are the solutions.

You don't need a set of rigid rules to win at love; you simply need to understand and apply the universal truths and not forget them when your so-called Mr. Right walks through the door.

Sis, Don't Settle is a guide to activating every layer of vitality and greatness inside of you—and applying it to the relationships and life you envision. And as a guide, there will be a lot of practical advice on how to deal with peer pressure for not being in a relationship by a certain age, finding happiness in your singleness, Dating 101, how to become the right person to attract the right person, how to properly identify red flags, communication Dos and Don'ts (when to text or call), dealing with rejection, healing from toxic relationships, the sex factor, and much more, so that you stop dating creeps and drones, and end sucky relationship cyclones and roller coasters once and for all. You got this.

I want you to dig deeper into who you are so you can clearly define the life and love that you want. All of us have a limited number of years on earth. What do you want your relationships to look like? Not messy, right? How do you want to spend the precious moments you have ahead of you? Not on flakes. Who do you want to spend it with? Not with someone who you have to beg to be there. When you've done the proper self-assessment, you will choose better, and instead of falling in love, you'll walk into it with your eyes wide open. Make a well-informed, purposeful, smart decision to go down a relationship path with the Forever Love you deserve. Having such a grand vision for your life gives it special meaning. It makes the journey all the more fun and interesting because of who you will become on your way. We never arrive in life. We simply reach milestones. I am going to help you reach this one—after reading this book, you'll never settle in love again. You'll attract the love you deserve.

I don't presume to be the ultimate expert on relationships, but I have dealt with thousands of women on the issues in their relationships— women from all demographics, cultures, circumstances, and situations—during my years as a judge on *Judge Faith* and *Divorce Court* and prior to that in my decade-long practice in New York that included family court. As a result, I'm acutely aware of where women make choices that are not in their heart's best interest. I've also been dating, relating, breaking up, and making up for a long time too (before I married). I've made some of the same mistakes as people in my courtroom. (Yes, girl, I did orchestrate that full-on search and seizure of my news anchor boyfriend's apartment, when he was out of town on vacation. SMH. Forgive me.)

You can be successful in your career and a failure in matters of the heart. You can be a smart person in life, yet clueless in love. As women, we often learn this the hard way. We're all human, with hungry hearts. We all make mistakes. To be truly smart and successful in relationships, we have to learn from them.

My job is to be the judge—and I've given raw feedback, served straight without any chaser to people who've heeded my advice and managed to change their lives for the better. Unlike a therapist, who takes years to get to the heart of a patient's bad choices, I call my litigants out on theirs in the moment, and I tell them exactly how they've screwed up and how to fix their lives moving forward. This book may not be for everybody. Some women want shortcuts and quick fixes to lock down their latest F-boy—this book is not that. We're past hook-ups. If you're reading this book, you're a woman looking for something different (or a man trying to understand what accomplished and successful women want out of life and love). Either way: you're in the right place.

No settling starts here right now.

Let's Make a Pact

Ladies, understand that you are the protagonist of your own story, and it's time you gave yourself permission to have the love you desire in your life. If that includes a loving, healthy marriage, then that's exactly what you can have. But you have to start being smart when it comes to matters of the heart.

Sis, Don't Settle is a pledge that I'd like you to make to yourself right now. I want you to promise yourself that you will hold out for the love you want because I know, if you put the principles of this book into practice, you will attract that love. However, like Mandy Hale said, "Hope for love, pray for love, wish for love, dream for love...but don't put your life on hold waiting for love." When you commit to a life of love you are also committing to courageously examining what makes you uniquely you. This then lets you take the next step of extending that love outside of you.

So here's our pledge:

I am attracting the highest, truest love into my life.
This person is loving, loyal, inspiring, and kind.
I continue to remain grounded and keep my heart open.
I walk away from anything and anyone that doesn't serve me.
I start over as often as is necessary because I'm not starting from
    scratch, I'm starting from experience.
From every experience, I grow healthier and mature.
I pledge to live now, not wait.
I am committed to excellence in all areas of my life.
I continue to get better mentally, physically, and spiritually.
I honor and cherish myself and those all around me.
I am becoming the best version of myself and attracting someone
    doing the same.
For this, I will not settle.

Part I

—⧆—

IT'S ALL ABOUT YOU

Chapter 1

"Just Pick Someone Already." No!

"Your task is not to seek for love, but merely to seek and find all the barriers within yourself that you have built against it."

—RUMI

Ally McBeal was a television series that ran on Fox from 1997 to 2002 about a young Harvard-educated attorney who joined a prestigious law firm where her childhood sweetheart and first love also worked. As an aspiring attorney myself I watched regularly—I loved the glitz and grit of the legal dramas. In 1999, in a promotion to tease the next episode, the network ran an ad: "Tonight, Ally's worst nightmare! She turns thirty. And she's single." Ally's worst nightmare wasn't falling from the top of the Empire State Building, or realizing in the midst of jury arguments she had on two different shoes, or accidentally cc-ing her boss on an email gripe about work. Nope. It was being single at thirty.

Everywhere we turn there's messaging being sent to single women about how questionable it is to not be married by a certain age. It's exhausting hearing about so many relationships that failed because someone felt pressured (whether from outsiders or internally) and made poor decisions based on an artificial timeline.

> *First comes love.*
> *Then comes marriage.*
> *Then comes Mary with a baby carriage.*

I was seven years old when I first started singing this song with the girls in my class in elementary school. Already at that age we were being ~~brainwashed~~ pressured to believe that there would be this natural order to love in our lives.

So when love came (and went)...when marriage didn't happen (or last)...when children weren't produced, our inner seven-year-old selves started questioning our entire life's trajectory and purpose.

I've never desired a love that felt like crossing something off a list. I'm a small-town girl but I've always dreamed big, and it never sat right with me (even from a young age) that I might be expected to sacrifice quality for speed. I wanted a love as deep as the ocean and as strong as Gorilla Glue with nothing but room to keep growing, and I'm sure you've felt that way too. There are a million ways society tells us that we need to stop being so "picky" if we want a man, but I've never subscribed to that. Some of the best things to happen in your life will not be on your schedule.

Now before we dive into the nitty-gritty (because, trust me, I have lots of opinions on and advice for dating), it's important that you know the Faith outside of the courtroom and TV glam. By all accounts, like any girl with strict parents, I lived a pretty sheltered life growing up in Louisiana. My dad was pretty laid back, but my mom? School, sports, church, and no boys was her motto. I was a good child, and so I stuck to mom's plan. In eighth grade I became a serious fast-pitch softball player. In tenth grade I joined the varsity cheerleading team. My social life went from after-school practices to homework to helping mom cook dinner. In college, I barely dated because I could never find the time. I used to joke that we had 400 clubs on campus and I belonged to 350 of them. In law school, nothing changed: I was keenly focused on my studies and graduated valedictorian of my class. I'd mastered certain areas of my life but, like a lot of young women, I was naïve about others—especially when it came to love.

In my last year of law school, I got offered a job at a big New York law firm. When I told my parents I'd be moving to New York City, my dad was thrilled. My mom cried. Moving to New York from Louisiana was a big stretch for me culturally, and the Big Apple's social scene was beyond this Louisiana girl's wildest dreams. I was in awe of the city, the tall buildings, the culture, the food—but most of all, the pace. I would meet people from all over the world, and they all seemed to be racing through New York City streets to the beat of their own drums. I felt a keen sense of accomplishment just being in the mix of it all. Step one and two to acclimating to my new life as a fresh New Yorker were to get a subway card and find an apartment. I found a beautiful place on the Upper East Side in Manhattan and learned how to commute on the train to work. I was officially adulting in the greatest city in the world. Step three was the next big step in my adult life: I wanted to share my new life and experiences with someone special. I was ready for love. I had a list of restaurants that had been featured on *Sex and the City* that I wanted to go to; I had live concerts at Madison Square Garden to attend, ice skating at Central Park, and dancing the night away in the Meatpacking District on my agenda. I thought New York City would be the perfect place to complete my dream life with my husbae. The city truly felt like my oyster.

After the first few days of orientation at the firm, I went with some of my fellow first-year colleagues to a happy hour. Enter Kevin.

Immediately, Kevin seemed like the man of my dreams. A successful attorney, good looking, Ivy League–educated...he was *everything*! Smart, fine, and funny (I was laughing too hard at his jokes, though—you'd have thought Chris Rock had popped up in our group chat). He asked me out, and my heart nearly squealed. As we began seeing each other, I invested more and more time and energy into dating him. I daydreamed about him at work. I'd spend hours on the phone with my girlfriends gushing about him. I found a good hairstylist in New York, and made sure to see her weekly so that I'd always look good just in case he called for the next date. (When you stay ready, you don't have to get ready!) After a few dates, I could already see myself walking down the aisle to meet this man. So when he suddenly stopped calling me, I thought it could mean only one thing: something terrible must have happened and he was somehow incapacitated! Let me get ready to console my man for whatever it might be. What will I say to his poor mother when I see her at the hospital? It was so unfortunate that I'd be meeting her for the first time in such a stressful situation.

Then I saw a social media post of him hanging out watching sports with friends. He was *alive*. Not hospitalized. Not in a coma. Whoa. After days of waiting, and still no call from him, I started asking some of our mutual friends.

"Hey, I haven't heard from Kevin, everything okay?"
"Yeah, he's cool."

"Um, so how's Kevin?"
"Good."

This made no sense. According to *The Rules*, a dating book made popular by *Sex and the City*, we were supposed to be entering phase two of our dating cycle, and here he was diverting from the plan. Clearly there was some kind of system error, because he'd shown that he liked me. What wasn't to like? I decided to make it easy for him to recognize the error of his ways. About a month after our last conversation, I got a lead from a woman who worked at his firm that he was going to be at a legal conference in Washington, DC, that weekend. That was great news. I could go to the conference and "run into him." It would look like an innocent encounter. I went to Macy's and splurged on a couple of new outfits, some high heels, and did some extra lunges at night so my legs would look just right in them. I got my hairdresser Carla to give me a good blowout and got a mani-pedi. I imagined how I'd strike up a conversation with him when he realized how lucky he was that we just happened to be at the same conference at the same time. "Oh, hey, Kevin, good to run into you! What a coincidence!" Which would lead to us grabbing dinner that night, and then him asking me out again on our next date in New York. "I'm so happy you were still available to go out with me, Faith. Thank you so *much* for this opportunity!" That would lead to the beginning of our wonderful relationship. And that's exactly what happened...though not with him. I'd also end up with way more than I set out for.

One day during a lunch break as I was entering a restaurant, a guy was coming out whom I'd seen around at the conference. He stopped to introduce himself. Enter Brian.

We struck up a conversation, and I found out he also lived in New York. He too was an attorney just starting out working at a law firm like me. We exchanged info, and he contacted me later that night. We met up and talked for a couple of hours. I had seen Kevin around the conference, and he was pleasantly surprised to see

me there as expected. He didn't suspect a thing about Operation
Un-Ghost, but slow and steady would be the plan with him that
week. In the meantime, Brian seemed pretty great.

When I got back to New York, nothing had changed with Kevin.
Apparently he'd started seeing someone else and she too was at the
conference. When I found out I knew it was a wrap with him. So
Kevin was out, but Brian apparently was in. Brian was tall, educated, and the only person I'd met who actually looked good in one
of those oversize Steve Harvey pinstripe suits. So I thought why not?
Indeed, he seemed to do everything right in the beginning. Called.
Followed up. Asked me out on dates every weekend. Sent me flowers
to show he was thinking of me. I thought okay, maybe this could
be something. The consistency was refreshing, especially after how
strangely things ended with Kevin. But after a couple of months I
started to notice significant red flags. One day I sent some online
research to his email so I could work on his home computer and saw
inappropriate messages from another woman. I immediately asked
him what in the world was going on—he cried and said it was someone he'd met randomly and swore it would never happen again. It
did. He then became very controlling about my whereabouts—it
was almost as if he was projecting his own inability to be disciplined
in his dating life on me. I would work until ten p.m. and he'd be
angry—convinced I was up to no good, when I was just tired and
wanting to sleep and get ready for the next workday.

We dated for four stress-filled months. He presented himself well
initially, but in the end his insecurities, coupled with his need for
female adulation, were too much for me. So after four months of
these philosophies being revealed over that time, I ended it. When
I told him things weren't working out, he didn't take it well. I
soon learned that Brian and a bruised ego just didn't go together.
He would say things like "No woman has ever broken up with me

before" as if that was going to magically make me change my mind. When that didn't work, he then did everything he could to "punish" me. He flaunted other women in front of me. He started telling mutual friends and professional colleagues from the conference that I was possessive and controlling. That's weird, since I'd ended the relationship and wasn't taking *his* calls. And he wouldn't stop contacting me. I left him on read for an entire year and he was still trying to reach me. He was cruel, vindictive, and wanted me to pay for choosing not to date him anymore. He tried to ruin my peace and my good name at work with my colleagues too.

I would often cry in regret, wishing that I had never met him that day coming out of that restaurant. I had uprooted my entire schedule to go to a conference to pursue Kevin, who clearly wasn't that interested in me. Had I just let that go I would never have met my biggest dating disaster—I mean, lesson. So those were the harsh realities of my initial dating experiences in New York. This was also the beginning of me realizing *something* had to give. It took time, growth, and a few more lessons, but eventually I decided: I was relentless in my academic pursuits and fiercely intentional about my career. Why should my romantic life get any less from me?

That *something* would reveal itself over the course of the next fifteen years. That was the amount of time I spent out in these dating streets! It was amazing to see how the dating world evolved from randomly meeting while out and about or being set up on blind dates (with not much to go on via Google), to the digital world taking over via dating apps or sites like Match.com, to social media meet-ups. In the end, rarely would people even exchange phone numbers anymore—they would simply follow each other on social media. And if they saw what they liked, they'd slide in the DMs. Technology added a whole new set of issues to the equation—calls turned to texts, ignoring turned to left on read, dates turned to swiping right.

Keeping someone's attention and knowing where you stand became harder than ever. Technology also added two more elements that were game changers when it came to the opposite sex: access and temptation.

At some point I learned through trial and error that patience would be the key to success on my love journey. I had no time for draining boyfriends or chasing after someone.

I told myself it would all work out with my love life and I should live the rest of my life to the fullest no matter what. That would be easier said than done.

What I learned as I navigated the dating world is that my experiences in love—the disappointments, the heartbreaks, and the resultant walls I put up—weren't unique to me. I was like a lot of women, trying to navigate uncharted territory, learning lessons the hard way, and going through the same ole situations. I decided there had to be a better way than this treadmill cycle of dating. Patience needed to be my new mantra. Good things come to those who wait, right?

While I was proud of my newfound perspective on dating, it wouldn't be long until I found myself questioned by my friends, family, and men: why are you still single? They wanted to know what I was waiting for. The constant assumptions that I lacked something in my personality or character or that I was intentionally preventing myself from finding my soulmate would irritate me and then chip away at me sometimes. It felt like they just wanted me to pick someone already! I'd been around plenty of women who had just "picked someone," and I was not impressed. Over time, my experiences would prove the importance of my decision not to rush.

There are few other choices that will leave as many footprints along your life path as who you connect yourself with emotionally, spiritually, and physically. You can pick a dress. A hairstyle. A bag. A restaurant for dinner. Those decisions will rarely change the course of your life or be moments that you regret even years later. But you can't just pick a man. Not one that you expect to have a healthy, emotionally intelligent, long-term relationship with.

You'll make all kinds of choices on your relational path. These choices will not be as easy as you'd think. They require you making a decision that your future self will either thank you for or wish she could go back in time to shake some sense into you. If the decisions you make are smart, you'll see the result in your heart.

There's nothing more gratifying than a healthy, loving, committed relationship with someone you admire, love, and trust. A person with whom you can share your innermost thoughts and feelings. Someone who has your back and you have theirs. A person who sticks by your side through thick and thin—in life's ups and downs. Through the fire and the storm. That kind of companionship is one of life's greatest gifts, and this book is the beginning of your journey to unwrap it.

The cost of that dress? $50.
The cost of that bag? $200.
The cost of dinner at the restaurant? $150.
The cost of Forever Love: priceless.

Chapter 2

Single (and Thriving!) in the City

"You are your best thing."

—TONI MORRISON

Singleness is a full and whole experience, not a rest stop.

So say it loud, ladies:

I'm single and I'm proud.

And I promise not to settle...

Fast forward ten years since the Brian/Kevin saga...I was celebrating my thirty-fifth birthday with family and friends and not a man in sight. In the South, where I grew up, having never been married before forty was as unnatural as seeing a dog walk on its hind legs. As bizarre as going to the beauty shop on Saturday and leaving before five p.m. or, God forbid, as awful as Pastor Wilkins cussin' during the Sunday sermon. And I don't say this to exaggerate—there was nothing subtle about how people weighed in on my love life. I'll never forget this one time when I was hanging out with friends from New Orleans who had become very successful musicians. We had known one another for several years, yet when we ran into one another at an event, one of the guys said, "You're still single?! Oh, you must be crazy." He knew me well enough to know I'm not the crazy type at all and yet still thought it was both funny and appropriate to make such a comment in a group of all our friends. I'm sure he wasn't intentionally trying to hurt me, but the comment stung nonetheless, in part because it wasn't my first time hearing it.

Another moment that sticks out for me was a comment made years ago underneath an Instagram post I made. I had shared a photo with my friend's cat, and a commenter wrote, "Can't even get a man lol." *Ouch. Jeez.*

I had to thicken my skin and get comfortable ignoring the trolls. It really isn't anyone else's business for you to explain your personal life journey, but I know the questioning probably comes for you too. That's why you have my full permission to answer these silly questions about your singleness with snark, sass, sarcasm, or all of the above.

Why Are You Single? Five Sassy Responses

1. I'd like to invite you to become a member of "Mind Your Business Ministries." Would you like to join?
2. I didn't realize I needed a reason.
3. I'm actually in a relationship—with my freedom.
4. Why? Well, according to my married friends, it's because I'm lucky!
5. I'm overqualified, but let's see what the newest applicants will bring.

If you're not careful about uploading all of those negative insinuations about being single, you may begin to feel like somehow your singledom means that something must be wrong. Being "still single" can start to feel like it's something to be embarrassed about. Or feel like despite whatever you've accomplished it doesn't matter, because life is incomplete or that somehow you've failed if you don't have a man. Unfortunately, that attitude makes many single women internalize low self-worth. And this is when the ugly faces of settling and desperation begin to show up—when you begin to believe that singlehood is a byproduct of something off within you, you begin to operate as though you're lucky that ole boy is slightly interested. These messages get nice and comfortable within our minds, reiterating that "beggars can't be choosers" and that we deserve what life hands us.

Once that cycle of harmful thoughts begins, it's extremely difficult to undo. There's not much others can do to convince you that you deserve all the good things life has to offer when your track record with the opposite sex says otherwise. There is nothing your friends or family could truly say—you have to believe it for yourself and interrupt the lies you've been telling yourself about what happiness truly feels like. Being alone doesn't need to mean that you're lonely, but the messages circling around me were intent on reminding me that my accolades and achievements couldn't keep me warm at night and that despite my professional advancement I was still "just" a single woman at the end of the day.

What starts off as snarky comments and feelings of loneliness can quickly spiral into a "zone of danger." In law, the zone of danger rule states that you are at risk of physical harm or emotional distress by how close you are to a crime. For example, being almost hit by a car or watching a loved one get hit by a car puts you in the zone of danger because you could have been scathed. In the context of this discussion about being single, I believe the societal pressures on women to become married spiral out of control, becoming a zone of danger if you aren't careful. Next thing you know you can find yourself making bad romantic decisions that change the trajectory of your life, all because you were taken in by the pressure to get married or get a boyfriend. I see it *all* the time on *Divorce Court*, where beautiful, smart women put their careers, children, and financial health on the line. And though they may think they are doing it for love, it's not love at all but rather the pressure to keep a relationship, even if it causes you to settle for less.

I want to help all of my sisters stay out of this zone of danger because it operates just like quicksand: easy to get caught up, hard to get out.

Let Go of "The Lie"

You have to make a decision. Make a decision right now that you will reject any thoughts, ideas, words, or notions contrary to your truth. You can't change small-minded or ignorant people who may think something is wrong with you because you're single. *Oh, you broke up, what did you do now? You still can't bring a date to the party? Maybe you should try harder.* These people are hazardous, so ignore them, please. You should never listen to the crowd. There's a reason they're in the crowd. You don't have to explain your singledom to people anymore, you don't have to justify it, you don't have to argue about it. What you do have to do now is make a choice to let go of the lie.

The lie is that nagging feeling that tells you that being single is a season of your life that you should get out of ASAP. It tells you that your really annoying aunt who shows up, along with her watery mac and cheese, to ask you every Thanksgiving, "Why aren't you married yet, girl?" is right and you're a loser. You believe this lie even though you have a great career, wonderful friendships, excellent credit, or other things that fulfill your life and bring you pride. Even if all of those things are works in progress, you're learning your happiness is never tied to anything outside of yourself. The truth is, wasn't Adam single before he met Eve, auntie? Aren't *all* people single before they get into a relationship? Therefore, it's ridiculous to feel like you should feel bad or ashamed about being single, because your life path is different from what others expect. Being intentional with the way you *think* and what you *say* about being single is the first step to not settling. Don't let anyone tell you what your story should be. You make your own story. You're not adhering to any arbitrary deadlines. Tell whomsoever asks questions, "I got this."

Your Time to Fly (and Be Fly)

When I tell women this, they get excited about the prospect of living their best lives in the now. Then they call me and ask, "Well, what am I supposed to do on Friday nights? I ain't got nobody." I have answers.

There is no better time to explore and try new things than when you're single. Make a major career shift, take those dance classes you've been thinking about—the ones your ex called a waste of time. Take off to Rome for a two-week cooking class. There is no one stopping you! Go where you want to go. Be who you are called to be. Remember, there are things you can do when you're single that you might have to negotiate when you're in a relationship. Your significant other may not find it fun to move to Bali for a year. Binge-watch trashy TV, eat Pringles in bed late at night with a deep-moisturizing face mask on (while binge-watching), do all the lazy things you want on Saturdays and take advantage of not having any other person there to observe it. Go on a last-minute road trip to the vineyard with your girlfriends and splurge on shoes without the judgment from a frugal lover. For the most part your future partner will not be a photocopy of you, and adjustments or conversations or negotiations will be needed, but not right now! Currently it's all about you!

When I moved to New York, my life became an amazing adventure. In addition to learning my craft as an attorney, I suddenly had a fun life with friends, travel, great restaurants, dancing, and Broadway shows. It was pretty common for my New York friends in their twenties, thirties, and even forties to be single. We were living such busy, fulfilling lives in the greatest city in the world, no one was checking for a biological clock. We were thriving! I worked hard toward the life I had built for myself, and constantly being questioned about the lack of a man in it wasn't helpful nor getting me married any quicker. People were trying to force me into a competition I didn't want to be in.

I learned so much during my single years about my independence. (Remember, I was brought up basically chained to my books.) While single, I realized the beauty of sheer autonomy—there were no one's expectations to meet but my own. I traveled alone and often, to places like Paris, Berlin, and Austria. On one trip, I went to Poland and took a bus with other tourists to the Auschwitz concentration camp. Passing under that gate was an incredibly solemn moment. I had read about it in history books, but there was nothing like being at the site. It was such an emotional experience, and I really connected with several people in our tour group. We talked a lot about how we were impacted by our visit and what we learned. On those trips, I was forced out of my comfort zone, and I met way more people than I would have if I had been with friends or a partner. I

stretched myself, became more independent, and in turn I grew—
stronger, more confident, and more aware.

Even if you don't have the funds to travel, there are a million
other cool things you could do right at home. You could volunteer
to use your time to help others, learn how to cook and start having
dinner parties of your own, or take your favorite niece or nephew on
surprise adventures. I'll discuss this in detail later, but this is how
I met my husband, and I've heard the same from countless other
women. They were trying something new and different—pursuing
hobbies and interests, living their best single lives—and in the midst
of doing so, there he was.

If your goal is to marry, how you live as a single person will dramatically impact your chance for relationship success when you meet
the "right" person. You can bypass a mountain of unnecessary pain
and regret if you use this time to learn about your self and to become
a better you who will, in turn, attract a better them. Embrace this
and choose to thrive in it. Think of it as your prerequisite to coupled
life. Before I could become an attorney, I had to enroll in a certain
curriculum, take the classes, and pass the bar exam. There were levels to it. There were mistakes and lessons learned to make me wiser,
smarter, and stronger. The same goes for finding a life partner. We're
often so eager to stop being single that it becomes a time we dread,
instead of a time to grow and fully enjoy. It's human nature to crave
companionship, but until you learn who you really are and what
you want and need, you won't be successful in a relationship, and
you will only have wasted time. You will have wasted years of a life.
When you're single, you're in a special mindset where your priority
is you and becoming a better you. Don't ever let anyone rush you
through this—you have skills to hone and life tests to pass. *(And fun
to have, of course!)*

Many of my friends in Louisiana were married and had kids at thirty. It was beautiful to see them growing families and finding love early. But that wasn't my story. And I still absolutely loved my life. Unfortunately, the world doesn't always believe that women can be happy outside of a relationship, especially those over a certain age. I still found myself confronted with so many misconceptions about single women. One year my mom's neighbor had seen me on TV doing legal commentary. During a visit, I saw her, and she said hello, and I'm not exaggerating when I say that the very next words out of her mouth were, "Why aren't you married?"

I immediately said, "Because I'm living out my journey, and no one else's." I wasn't being flippant. Well, maybe a little. I knew she needed that membership to Mind Your Business Ministries, but this was a perfect example of how even when I was certain that I was living my best life, I was still battling with how to prove my happiness to others. Once a month I would get a comment or direct message from someone who had seen me on television asking me about my relationship status. One woman wrote to me angrily and said, "It's time for you to get married and have children!" Why this stranger cared so much about my personal life, I'll never know, but the internet is full of people who just refuse to mind their business.

I ultimately came to terms with the fact that those statements actually say more about the person who said them than they do about me. I had to learn to ignore, delete, and let it go in one ear and out the other. Are the people who are pressed for you to have the status of "married" helping you prepare for what it takes to be successful in marriage? No. So you must not give their passing judgments any power. I was in several relationships over the years and would never post or share about them publicly despite getting questions about my marital status. Why? Because I am comfortable in my journey and didn't feel the need to prove my worth by validating my relationship status to anyone else.

You're not on anyone else's timetable, so don't sit out living your life because you're on someone else's life map to connect with yours. There's no need to waste precious years waiting on a plus-one to enjoy yourself. If you believe in God, the Universe, or the divine, then leave the life maps to them. They are better than the metro in making connections. Time is going to pass anyway; your life is on a clock and it doesn't stop even for you. We only have but so much time on this Earth to enjoy ourselves—why not love life for every moment that you can.

Are Married People *Really* Happier?

I know we're just getting into dating, but let's think about marriage. (*Slow your roll, Faith*, right? Well, just give me a second of your time.) A lot of people have marriage on a mountaintop; they are climbing and trying to conquer it. And once they get to this mountaintop, they believe that's where life really unfolds for them: marriage, family, and security. Until then, they're striving to get there. Their success and happiness are tied to succeeding at that. Marriage is not the magic equation for achieving fulfillment in your life. If you're not happy alone, you won't be happy with someone else either. In fact, many people choose not to marry, and that choice should be respected. Their lives aren't lacking in excitement or joy, and they've found love in other relationships—whether it's romantic companionship or with family and friends. We assume that anyone who could be married would be, when the reality is some are opting out.

A good friend of mine, Keli, and her boyfriend, Tim, had been dating four years. Keli is an attorney in Dallas. We met at a house party one night when I was in town celebrating a mutual friend's birthday. I was immediately drawn to her bubbly personality, and we hit it off right away. She was beautiful, smart, Ivy League–educated, and—in true Southern belle fashion—as sweet as pie. Later that year, Keli confided in me that she was ready for Tim to propose. He was thirty-two years old, well established in his career, and they had a happy relationship. Keli had broached the subject with Tim several times, but he wasn't budging—he told her the truth about how he felt. He simply didn't want to get married. Keli had spent the last two years of their relationship hoping she would change his mind, but to no avail. Keli ended things with Tim amicably, although it hurt like hell. But she respected his choice. Tim told me he wasn't afraid of marriage or commitment and that Keli was really amazing. He just knew he wasn't ready. Anyone would respect his authenticity. It's hard to stand in your truth when you're being pressured by family and friends or even strangers who refuse to mind their business. Tim knew at thirty-two what so many people struggle for years to learn: that everyone's journey in life is different, and that's okay. He knew that the choice to make a lifelong marriage commitment was a deeply personal decision only he could make if it was going to be Forever Love.

Marriage is not for everyone. For some, marriage is not for right now (they are still figuring out life on their own). Not being married can be the result of a number of things, including a personal choice not to marry! For some women, marriage is not on the list at all. Successful women like Shonda Rhimes and Oprah have talked about their choice to stay unmarried. Rhimes said that as a young girl she always knew she wanted kids, but she never wanted to marry because she valued her freedom too much. Oprah has never married her longtime beau Stedman Graham, and she's out there getting lifetime achievement awards, running a media empire, and having tea with Meghan Markle. There is no reason to feel like these women are lacking, just because they haven't married.

Dr. Indra Cidambi, a medical doctor focusing on mental health, has said, "Being alone does not make a person lonely, but the perception of being alone is what makes one lonely." An *Oprah Daily* article titled "The Surprising Benefits of Being Single" showed that studies prove unmarried people are healthier and make more time for friends than married people. Married people experience a bump of happiness at the beginning of the marriage, but then it goes back to where people were before they got married. What does this mean? I'm by no means telling you that marriage sucks (it's incredible when you put in the work!), but that marriage and relationships are not a method of escape. It's not a way to solve your loneliness. There's no man who can fix you and, in fact, the wrong man can hurt you deeply.

Some of the saddest times of my life were when I was in an unhappy relationship, and some of the happiest times were when I was single and focused on myself. It all comes from within. So the choice is really yours. What will your perspective be? If I had caved to those people pressuring me or trying to make me feel bad about not being married, I would be somewhere else right now—married and unhappy, or even divorced.

When you are confident in your life wherever you are on your life path—single or not—it speaks to your wholeness as an individual. There is no need to strive for completion from an outside source when you have what you need from within. Wanting companionship is a valid and beautiful life goal. But understand that companionship should only add value to your *already* high-value life.

Chapter 3

Unapologetically Top Shelf

"Love yourself first and everything falls into line."

—LUCILLE BALL

My sophomore year in college I was a member of the dance team at Louisiana Tech University—the Regal Blues, as they are now called. I didn't have a car, so I would often ride with other girls from the squad or friends to and from football games that were off campus. One night I was in the back seat, and we were exhausted from cheering all night at the game. Our team had lost—in fact we were commiserating on how they got beat like they stole something before eventually we fell silent and the radio filled the space. Something about the Brian McKnight song "Crazy Love" being played made me feel reflective. I looked up at the stars through the sunroof and instinctively thought, *Somewhere out here in this world is my husband*. Interestingly, I was not one of those college girls harping on her MRS degree. I wasn't one reading *Black Bride* magazine from cover to cover or who'd had my wedding dress picked out since age twelve. In fact, I was so focused on school I wasn't even interested in having a boyfriend. So it was such a random thought to me at the time—it wasn't a reaction to anything that was being discussed in the car or something that had happened that day. But at that moment, I wondered what he was doing.

I didn't know it would take twenty years before I met him. I would go through a lot of peaks and valleys in my life over the course of the next two decades. But eventually I came to the conclusion that I knew who I wanted him to meet. How I chose to live my life now mattered because it was the version of me that he'd see when we first set eyes on each other. It would impact what I said during our first conversations. Would he meet a healed and whole Faith or an angry, depressed, crazed, unfulfilled me who had been dragged and wounded due to broken relationships? I didn't want to be a carbon copy of other women either. I wanted to be unique and distinctive. I wanted to know myself more and what I liked and what I didn't—to understand my feelings about certain topics. Singlehood was not my curse, it was my time of preparation and evolution.

Around this time was when I began to internalize what it meant to be a high-value woman who attracts quality over quantity. If I wanted to be unique and distinctive, I had to do something unique and distinctive. I couldn't just show up to restaurants featured in movies hoping to see my idyllic love walk through the door on cue. Suddenly the "work" of love made sense: it starts long before you actually begin dating. What did it mean to be valuable? What did it mean to love the skin I'm in? What did it mean to find someone to share happiness—not make me happy? The more I could build up my high-value self, the more I would draw in someone of high value to share my life with.

Smart women don't settle in their careers, friendships, or even with their hairstylist, so why would we settle in love? When that thought set in, I began to truly understand that the journey to

Forever Love would begin with Me. First, knowing that I deserved the best and then, secondly, defining what matters most to me. My journey to authentic love didn't start with finding the right person; it started with loving the person at the center of it all—me—and becoming *my* best version of myself.

Michelle Obama chose *Becoming* as the title of her memoir because she said it was reflective of her journey of becoming her. She emphasized how being intentional about learning at every step of her life path better prepared her for what was next. Preparation was the key.

If I wanted to do well on an exam in school, I studied. I didn't just show up with holy water to sprinkle on my papers hoping I'd get the answers through osmosis. If athletes want to win a game, they practice. They work out. They exercise. They eat food that fuels their stamina. They don't just show up at game time snacking on a two-piece spicy after binging Netflix all week saying, "Put me in, coach!"

Preparation dramatically increases your chances for success in every area you pursue in life, including your relationships. Finding or attracting the right person is great. But that's only part of the process. If you're not prepared for their presence in your life, it's all for naught.

How do you prepare? It starts with bringing a healthy you into the equation. You want to meet the right person, correct? You have a list of what you want? That's great. Your dream person likely does too. Would they be excited about meeting you? To prepare for the relationship you want, you must be as intentional about becoming the right person as you are about attracting the right person.

A healthy relationship is made up of two healthy people. I'm not talking about people who have it together all the time—I'm referring to the ones who actively seek out their best selves and continue to work on *becoming* better all along the way.

People who work on becoming the best version of themselves understand:

If they know how to effectively communicate, it will be reflected in their relationships. If they know how to manage their emotions, it will show in their relationships. If they know how to create boundaries, it will show in who they choose to connect with. If they refuse to make someone else responsible for their happiness, their relationship will mirror that.

When you can see through healthy, healed, and whole eyes, you approach dating with a clearer vision. When your vision is clear, you create a path for better experiences and people to find you. It all starts with your preparation to become better.

How we speak to people, how we manage conflict, how we apologize, how we show compassion, how we sit in humility, and how we leave clothes on the floor, or dishes in the sink, or the toilet seat up will be the same whether it's in our own company or the company of someone else. This is why it is so important to *become* the right person to attract the right person.

So, I started becoming.

From this clarity came a calm resolve, and I was committed to holding out for exactly what I knew I wanted. Becoming takes time. It took time for me to figure out what that was, but eventually I became more confident in saying no to everything that wasn't that. No to not being made a priority. No to being ignored or not called back. No to not being cherished. No to insecurity. No to dimming my light so he doesn't feel threatened. No to disrespect. No to dishonesty. No to less than the best. No to counterfeit love.

And yes to honoring myself in becoming a high-value woman deserving of a high-value man.

A high-value woman holds herself in high regard and expects nothing less from her partner. Some call her bougie, but it's not about living an expensive lifestyle or having a self-aggrandizing attitude, but rather knowing that everything she does and everyone in her life serves an important purpose. She's not about being hard as nails or rigid or a "prude." She intrinsically knows her worth and uses that as her guiding light from which all her relationships will build.

The inner you that generates high-value love is the same place that attracts genuine love from others. If your inner source is unclear, your ability to attract high-value love is obscured. In order to bring light to that inner you, you will first need to learn how to give yourself what you are seeking.

Love creates more love.
The loving attract love.

When your own inner love light shines, you open yourself up to experience the beautiful wonder of a deep and powerful connection with another human being.

What else happens when you appreciate yourself for the high-value woman that you are? You start to attract high-value men who love women who know their worth. Becoming a high-value woman starts with appreciating the value in you.

Marsha kept seeing her boyfriend, Jay, constantly liking photos of Instagram models on social media and started feeling bad about herself. She started internalizing his likes as if they were indicative of deficiencies within herself. "I don't look like any of the women in the photos he likes. Maybe that's what he really prefers," she said to me. "He's settling for me." Marsha had gained twenty pounds during the pandemic and quarantine and wasn't feeling like her best self. Marsha, Marsha, *Marsha*. What I saw in front of me was a gorgeous woman—from the inside out, impeccable style, the best curves. And she was falling into the social media un-reality trap. I told her, "Sis, the Instagram models don't even look like the Instagram models. Take those five filters off those pics and you couldn't pick 'em out of a lineup." We might as well start singing the theme song from *Aladdin*, "A Whole New World," because there are too many folks who are a whole different person without that airbrushing and manipulation. But even if that weren't the case, Marsha needed to know: comparison is the thief of joy.

First, I agreed with her that it was disrespectful for Jay to like photos of scantily clad women once she told him that she wasn't comfortable with it, but more than that—Marsha had to stop defaulting to questioning her own self-worth over her boyfriend's Insta-happy fingers or the twenty pounds she wanted to lose. Even though she decided to end the relationship because she and Jay weren't on the same page, she knew she had some work to do. Often our triggers reveal the places we need to heal. As for Jay, it appears he also had a lesson to learn: often the grass is greener on the other side...because it's fake.

Second, we're our own worst critics when it comes to our perceived flaws. So many of these negative inner conversations take a toll on our self-worth. It blocks the path to loving ourselves outrageously, like no one else could. If you're waiting to be prettier, thinner, richer, smarter to feel better about yourself and think that's when you'll attract a high-value partner, you're missing out on precious time and love in the now.

You'll never get to "perfect." Perfect is a race—and as you run toward it, the finish line keeps moving farther away. You don't have to be perfect to be loved—you have to be you. A high-value woman knows this.

To become a high-value woman you have to nurture the relationship you have with yourself. Just like in any relationship, we don't expect that relationship to be the same from day to day. Most of us usually expect there to be ebbs and flows and changing seasons in our friendships, family relationships, and romantic interests, but the same is true for the relationship we have with ourselves. When you learn to love yourself, you have a lifelong romance that never fades or tires you. And when you know your self-worth, everyone else will know it too.

Here are some scenarios to show the difference between low-value and high-value self-worth.

Dating Scenario	Low-Value Response	High-Value Response
He won't commit.	Give him an ultimatum.	Pull away because he is holding up the line.
You're confused about where you stand.	Demand an answer.	Knowing that if you have to ask, you already know the answer.
He calls once every two weeks.	Get angry because he didn't call sooner.	Didn't notice. Too busy living your best life.
He asks you out on a date day-of and you already have plans.	Turn into Simone Biles bending over backward to clear your schedule.	#bookedandbusy. Kindly thank him for the invite and take a rain check.

High-value self-worth comes with knowing what you love about yourself. Many of us are so quick to acknowledge our flaws but not to tell ourselves enough about all the good. On a daily basis most of us take for granted our accomplishments and positive attributes. Don't nitpick at yourself: society is already doing enough of that. Instead of overthinking that baked chicken you overcooked (again), focus on the fact that at least you tried, and love yourself some more.

If you didn't get the laundry done, but you made it through your workday, love yourself some more. If you only worked out once this week, that's more than zero! We're all a work in progress, but your job is to amplify your positives as you continue to grow in other areas. Nurture your inner being. You completed that work project on time. You read that book *Sis, Don't Settle*, which was nourishment for your soul. You have moments of progress every day. Show yourself grace.

Here's what my "self" has enjoyed hearing from me:

I am smart.
I am talented.
I am strong.
I am love.
I am living a life that I don't need a break from.
I have friendships that I don't have to question and relationships that I don't have to fake.
I am not waiting until marriage to be the woman I was called to be.

What does your self want to hear? Ask yourself this often. Just like in any relationship, loving yourself fully requires time, attention, care, and practice. This relationship acts as a template from which all the love alliances in your life are shaped. Setting the quality, tone, and standard for how another person loves you starts with how well and how deliciously you love yourself. Tell yourself sweet things, be gentle and kind to yourself, take yourself nice places, give yourself nice gifts. How you relate to yourself signals to others how they should relate to you. The best way to communicate how to love you is to show people how you do it for yourself. By investing these good things in yourself, without any words necessary, it naturally establishes the working model of how you will receive love from others.

If a genuine love relationship is what you desire, learn to honor and cherish yourself as a special and lovable person. It is the cultivation of this relationship with self that will ultimately determine the success of other relationships.

If I asked ten women right now to describe what they are seeking in a man, the answers would vary from person to person—*Ooooh, at least six feet tall, six-figure income, and if not Michael B. Jordan himself, one of his brothers will do!* I hear ya, but if we dig a little deeper, there are several constants that would likely emerge. Most would say they want someone who is kind, thoughtful, respectful, who will make them feel special and valued, who will be a great listener, loves their family, and is an effective communicator, someone who will be an encourager and love you unconditionally for who you are.

If I were to ask each of them how many of these behaviors they currently extend to themselves, I could end up in a silent room.

Holding yourself in high regard and knowing in your heart that you are valuable and special means being kind, patient, gentle, and compassionate with yourself the way you would be with someone else you care about. It also means tuning in to your own wants and needs the same way you would want a partner to attend to you.

You're Better Than Bottom Shelf

Every day you unconsciously show and tell people how to treat you without ever saying a word. Everyone around you will look to you for guidance on how much love and respect you require. You give them the clues. You dictate how people speak to you, how they act toward you, and what they expect from you.

Case in point number one: China was thirty-two years old and upset in my courtroom one day because her boyfriend had not proposed after three years. He had also slept with two other women when they were on "breaks" during the relationship. China told me that they had agreed not to see people during those times apart—but that they were to use the time to reflect. She was devastated when she found out both times that he had become involved with someone else. She still accepted him back into the relationship—*both times*. I told her, of course he was going to keep doing his thing and keep coming back, because you had sent him an obvious message: that you'd allow it. He has no incentive to do anything different when you've never required it. He knew he didn't risk losing you.

Knowing your self-worth is the first step in teaching a guy how to treat you. Even when you don't know it, you are still teaching the guy. Case in point number two: Kendra was thirty years old and looked tired and frustrated when she appeared before me in court. She told me she was unhappy in her relationship and that things had taken a turn for the worse. She continued, and shared that she had never felt she was attractive, so when Christin became interested in her, she was thrilled. After knowing each other for only thirty days Christin proposed to Kendra, and she accepted the proposal. They got married, and things went downhill very fast. Christin was always highly critical of Kendra and her weight. He belittled her as a way to "motivate" her, she said. That would be short-lived, and soon he'd be feeding her deepest insecurities by regularly calling her fat, lazy, and a slob.

It's heartbreaking to see women stay in relationships where they are repeatedly disrespected. Over time a disrespected person will conclude that they are, in fact, unworthy of respect. It will start to feel normal. Routine. That's exactly what happened with Kendra.

I asked Kendra some basic questions about herself, and almost immediately her core truths started to reveal themselves. She was unhappy with her life, and so much of it was rooted in low self-esteem. When we discussed how she treated herself—with neglect and unkindness—she realized that the men in her life were almost mirroring her behavior. She thought very little of herself, and it was evident in her words and deeds. Her dating prospects had been jerks, but they'd also been responding to the message of what she thought was an acceptable way to treat her.

I squared in on Kendra and told her the bottom line: "What you believe about yourself will keep showing up in your life." Nothing will affect your desire to manifest the love you want in your life more than your core beliefs about the love you are worthy of. I continued: "My hope is that you won't spend another minute allowing anyone to treat you so poorly. And, Kendra, that includes yourself." What we believe about ourselves affect us in two ways: first, it dictates our own actions, and second, it creates an expectation in our own minds of how we believe we deserve to be treated.

If you believe you are unworthy of love, you will attract partners who treat you as if you are unworthy. If you treat yourself as unimportant, chances are you will be treated the same by other people in your life, including the men you date.

On the other hand, if you require respect, caring, kindness, and integrity in your relationship with yourself, you will lay the foundation to receive that from others. If you are forgiving to yourself, others will know it is not acceptable to berate you for your mistakes. If you respect your wants and needs, your partner will as well. Your inner beliefs and expectations will be reflected outward, and you will be treated in kind. But what about your flaws—how do you and others love those too?

Loving My High-Value Self

There's a popular hashtag on social media called #SelfLoveSaturdays. On this day your favorite platforms are flooded with notions about self-reflective love. Is it really that easy? To just love yourself? The truth is, we've all been hurt, and we've all dealt with things that have made us question ourselves and whether we deserve the love we desire. Some of us more than others! In addition, we deal with so much comparison daily—on social media, in advertising, on TV, and in music—that can make us question our own sense of worth. If you're over forty, the world tells you that your time for love and family is ticking away. If you're not a size two, the ads say you need to lose weight. They are wrong!

So how do I do it? you might ask. It takes practice. Daily. For a lot of people, learning to love every part of themselves is a lifelong process. It doesn't happen overnight or with a magic wand. It's more like learning to play a new instrument—the more you practice it, the better you are at it over time. And then you eventually master it: the art of unconditional love.

Unconditional love is love without terms and conditions. That doesn't mean it is a love without accountability but rather a love that recognizes you are a unique, fearfully and wonderfully made human. Practicing this kind of love on yourself is what will enable you to extend that level of tolerance in your relationships. If you accept your own imperfections, then you will be more understanding of the imperfections of others. If you learn from your own lessons, then you create room for others to learn and grow around you.

Why is this continual work on ourselves important? Because most couples don't have relationship problems, they have problems they bring into the relationship. Your relationship's health starts with the relationship you have with yourself.

As women we must love ourselves in every sense of the word. We work hard, take care of everybody (including Ms. Johnson's lawn), and we hold a lot of responsibility in the world. Here are a few of my favorite techniques for learning to give all the big love you give out to others back to yourself. These exercises may seem simple or feel funny at first, but they will have an impact right away on how you show up in the world with this positive perspective in your mind and in your heart. I like to do them in the morning, or before I start my day. Do them however you want, but do it. In fact, start doing them right now—why not?

1. Write down the compliments you received in the past day or week or month in a notebook. When you go back and read at the end of the week or month what nice things people had to say about you, you'll be pleasantly surprised by the list you've compiled. The purpose of this list is to shine your mental spotlight on the positive things people have observed about you to circumvent the automatic focus on the negative. The focus here is not to require validation or place a higher opinion of what someone else says above your own—rather, to appreciate the fact that people give you flowers every day. It's okay to smell them.

2. Do what makes you happy every day. What do you do that makes you feel recharged and rejuvenated? Make a list of the things that make you feel good and of how you treat yourself as special. Keep this list somewhere you'll see it daily, and commit to doing at least one act every day. Here are my top five:

   Walking outside in nature

> Taking a bubble bath
> Having coffee with a friend
> Meditating
> Listening to music

3. Affirm: Put this book down and go to the mirror and take a look. Tell yourself: "I love you. Wow. There is no one else on the planet like you." You may feel weird doing this, but it is critically important. It allows you to hear someone (you!) tell you those words out loud. So when you do hear "I love you" from someone else, you're not surprised, you're not in denial, you're not thrown for a loop—you believe it. The more you say this to yourself, the more you will soon recognize how much people start saying it to you. If you don't believe me, try it. Plant the seed of self-love, water it daily, and watch it grow in your life.

4. Affirm someone else. Remember when I said the loving will attract love? Life is a boomerang—the more energy you give to something, the more of it you will receive in return. If you want more love, start focusing on the loving aspects of everyone around you and affirming those aspects in people as often as you can. Just know the opposite of this is also true. The more energy you give to negativity, the more of it you see—if, for example, you are trolling people on social media, you are engaging in low vibrational behavior that high-value folks have no time for. Be so invested in your personal development and growth that you have no time for drama, gossip, or any habits that don't move you forward toward greatness.

A high-value woman goes into a relationship knowing she is not an incomplete half of a person without a relationship. So she looks to her partner to add to that already full and happy life. In other words, a high-value woman knows she *is* the one. So how she treats her man is an extension of how she has loved and treated herself.

When you stop searching for "The One" and start identifying yourself as "The One"—loving yourself in the way you've longed to be loved, and embracing your very own wholeness as an independent living and breathing being—you become the love you'll attract.

You are enough. That is the key to not settling in love. While the relationship is going to be key, it's only as strong as the two people who are in it. I know it's easier said than done, because as I discussed in the previous chapter, so many people have been conditioned to think that happiness comes from a plus-one instead of from within. But the sooner you realize that there is no mysterious soulmate out there who is going to complete you and make you happy, the sooner you will start to enjoy all the happiness in your life now.

Remember: there is only one person you are guaranteed to be with the rest of your life—that person is you. You are high-value. People may even call you high-maintenance. Well, when you're the one maintaining you, why is that a problem? Dust off your shoulders, readjust your crown, and act like you know!

Chapter 4

You Are "The One"

"Even if it makes others uncomfortable, I will love who I am."

—JANELLE MONÁE

You have to know the things you want in a relationship. The best way to know that is to know who you are. The high divorce rate I see every day in court may have less to do with bad marriages and more to do with people who made bad decisions, as a result of not giving enough thought to what they actually wanted while they were single.

When I decided to book a flight and pay for a whole conference that I had no interest in attending just to run into Kevin, who hadn't called me in over a month but was still posting gym selfies, that was a bad decision. A waste of my time. It's like I wanted concrete proof of what I already knew—he just wasn't that interested. But I had to see for myself. What I should have done was something so simple yet too profound for me to grasp at the time: let it go. Kevin was fine, but he wasn't that fine. I can hear the words coming out of my cousin Freda's mouth now: *Men are like buses—there's always another coming along!* Instead of setting standards for myself, I decided to become Detective Olivia Benson from *Law & Order* and investigate why he wasn't calling.

If you're constantly conforming when you meet someone new, it's a red flag. It means you don't really know yourself and what core values are important to you. Too many people get into relationships and get lost in the other person. You date an attorney, now you're watching reruns of *Suits* every night. You date a preacher, now you're in church at every service, when you haven't been since Easter 2015. You date a thug and now you belong to the streets. Instead decide, *Who do I want my Forever Love to meet?*

Let's make a few decisions right now. First let's decide *who you are.*

Place this book down, close your eyes right now, and think about the woman you are. You may have a good career, friends, and family. You may have things you're working on about yourself and ideas or areas of interest that you want to pursue. That's all part of who you are. For example, I am a daughter, a devoted believer, a mentor, a mentee, a singer, a dog mom, a pageant queen, an academic, a friend, and as a judge, a line of protection for the most vulnerable. Being fully aware of my fullness helps me see that anything added to my plate should be a bonus.

In the past, you've figured out what you want by dating, relating, and learning, essentially in a process of elimination. Sometimes you learn what you like by eliminating what you don't like. But there is also another way. As an attorney, you are taught to enter a negotiation knowing what you want and what you're willing to compromise on. In the heat of the moment, you might be talked down or miss out on something critical, simply by not having been prepared with what you want. Love is very similar, because you may become enamored of every gorgeous man without knowing what it is you're looking for inside. You have to take some time to get still and clear about what it is that you value, so you're not swept up by just your physical "type." Many happily married people I know will tell you their partner isn't anything like what they had previously considered their type, but that they were receptive to the heart and soul ties made.

Basically, you can't get what you want unless you know what it is. If you get in a car to go to a new clothing shop that you heard opened in town, you're probably going to use Google Maps or some other app to look up the directions. Using the navigation, you'll get to your destination and feel confident you're headed to the right place.

You wouldn't get in the car and just start driving around town hoping to find the store. You might drive by *a* store but not *the* store you actually want to go to. Without knowing what you want, you end up with *something* and may be content, but at best you'd be settling for whatever that is. At worst, you end up taking a wrong turn and leave with more of a headache than if you had just stayed home.

So how do you figure out what you want without all the mind fumble or having a dissertation on yourself? I've developed the Four Facts Method. You start by determining Four Facts about yourself.

1. **I am...**
   Define your values, fears, and desires in life.
2. **I need _____ in a life partner.**
   Make a list of your non-negotiables.
3. **I envision my life path as _____.**
   Dream here: what are your five-, ten-, and twenty-year plans?
4. **I bring _____ to my relationship.**
   Be clear on what you add so you can be a thoughtful partner—and no one can persuade you otherwise.

Knowing these Four Facts will make dating and choosing The One for you much more straightforward. By this I mean that you'll meet someone who gives you butterflies and is a perfect gentleman, but if he doesn't complement your Four Facts, it's a wrap. Just call Chipotle for a pickup, because he's not for you. This level of clarity can feel scary! Worrying that you're self-sabotaging and making a fuss about little things that don't matter is sure to be your next thought. But I'm here to tell you that the Four Facts do matter, because they are a reflection of the things that make you who you are. It's what you bring to the table, and if you try to overlook them now, you'll be addressing them later on.

Fact 1: I am...

Who are you? There is only one person who knows the secret to your success in lasting love. That person is you. To know you is to understand the essence of your being. You are in tune with all that makes you uniquely you. To know you is to understand what makes you happy or sad. What makes you cry. What drives your motivation or stifles it. What situations are or are not right for you and what you will and will not tolerate. What will you accept in the name of love? What will you reject in the name of love? This is where you become aware of your relationship expectations, your internal beliefs and issues. When you know who you are, you can align yourself with what you want rather than just going with the flow and following any trail that leads to nowhere.

It's only when you are in tune with yourself that you can know what you need. Smart choices for you in dating are grounded in knowledge of what love means and looks like to you. The more you know and understand yourself and your boundaries, the greater chance you have for success in your relationship. When you do your internal assessment, be true to yourself so that you can find a love who will be true to you as well.

This self-assessment takes time and honesty. For me personally, I started looking at my development as a person. I knew that I was caring and sensitive and that I would value that in someone else. I also knew my triggers and that I would never be satisfied by someone who was sloppy with commitment. For example, it was a turn-off when a man didn't call when he said he would, or was ambivalent about life. I recognized that I needed to be as clear as possible about what I wanted. I didn't care if it sounded crazy or far-fetched. There was something powerful about knowing exactly who I was and what I had to offer at that time in my life.

I then made a list.

Fact 2: I need…

One of my favorite biblical scriptures is this: *Write the vision down and make it plain* (Habakkuk 2:2). In college I'd write down my goals and dreams on note cards. I'd get very specific about what I wanted to accomplish; I wanted to graduate number one in my class from law school. I kept that card through my three years of law school and read it several days a week. I also did the work—I studied and learned the material and did due diligence to prepare for my test.

Writing it down made it concrete. It made it real. It caused me to really think about what I wanted and gave me clarity. When that vision came to pass and I graduated first in my class, I looked back at that note card and felt a great sense of accomplishment. I still have it to this day as a testament to what that clarity brought me.

Over the years I would make lists and then put them away and never look at them again. But with the last list I made about what I desired romantically, I made a list of fifty things I desired in a potential mate. I wrote them down and kept the list in a notebook so I could review it regularly. I made it a part of my routine to pull it out and reassess it. Just in case I was being too restrictive I put a catch-all at the end: *He will exceed the expectations I set for myself.*

It's good to know what you want and just as good to know what you won't live without in a relationship. Know your non-negotiables before even opening yourself up to the dating pool. These are the essential requirements that you are unwilling to compromise on. You simply can't live without these things in your partner.

On my list, loyalty and leadership were the biggest musts for me. I'm a busy woman and, as I mentioned, I need to be with someone whom I trust. Popping up at secret lunches and breaking into a locked phone aren't things I have time or energy for. That's not what happily ever after looks like and not something I am willing to compromise on. And while I'm clear on what I can't do, I also know what I'm capable of. I lead a life where I'm a boss. That's not a shameless plug but an honest observation. All day long I preside over a courtroom where I call the shots. When I get home, I want to be able to look to someone whom I can trust to lead us through difficult decisions.

Someone who thrives off drama or who makes poor decisions wouldn't be a good fit for me . . . and vice versa! It's likely that kind of man would feel a lot of pressure with someone like me. He would probably need someone who could hold his hand through areas that I simply don't have time or patience for. It's not that this kind of man is inherently a bad guy or that I'm too demanding. We just aren't compatible. Facts!

After you determine your non-negotiables, then decide, what is it that you desire? There are some universal benchmarks for what makes a good partner. Personality is different from character. Personality includes your outward behavior, like sense of humor and preferences; your character is your moral compass and internal qualities and beliefs.

There are key character traits to keep an eye out for to ensure you're spending time with someone capable of empathizing with and cherishing you.

My personal favorite character traits:

- **Cares about being a good person**—This sounds simple enough, but an alarming number of people spend their lives only looking out for themselves. They may do the occasional good deed for appearances, but they don't actually care to have a positive impact on the world and the people around them. People like this need deeper support to see themselves as part of a larger community worth caring about. It is possible to date someone successfully who has a narcissistic personality, but I suggest you run for the hills. No woman wants to assume the responsibility of teaching someone empathy when looking for a boyfriend.
  - o How do you know someone is a good person? Observe. Observe everything. In a bit we're going to discuss a Red Flag List, but even in earlier stages you should be making mental notes about what kind of integrity this person has and the subtle clues he's leaving behind. You've heard the saying: you can easily judge the character of a man by how they treat people who can do nothing for them. Pay close attention to how your man responds to those he perceives as "beneath" him. Those he perceives as vulnerable. Is his humility or good nature conditional? Because eventually

he will see vulnerabilities in you. The unkindness he shows to others is a part of who he is and won't disappear just because he's in a relationship.

o Also, listen to people who have come into contact with them. Besides your own observations, what do their colleagues, friends, family, and peers think about them? I'm not suggesting conducting a long-form survey, but just be open. Listen. Observe. You'll be surprised about what you can learn.

o This was one of the things I appreciated when I met my husband. Everywhere I went and on social media people had stories of how they had encountered him for years on end and he was always so kind to them—from hotel clerks to car drivers to his colleagues on the road.

o Always observe how people treat those around them—especially those they are not trying to impress.

- **Shares a fondness and admiration for you**—You love yourself, but it's also good to have a partner who prioritizes affection between you two. This way, down the line, you both can fall back on the love you share no matter what hardships or challenges present themselves. You should never have to second-guess whether your partner still *likes you,* so find someone intent on telling you how he feels and leaving nothing to interpretation.

o You want someone who is comfortable affirming their feelings for you. I'm not talking about looking for someone to validate your existence, but you do want your partner to be in touch with their own emotions enough to be comfortable discussing their feelings for you.

- **Willingness to share a life**—As you grow deeper into the relationship, building a shared identity within your relationship will be critical. *We* can be a difficult concept to grasp once you've been single for a long time, but it helps to have both parties feeling invested in the relationship's success.

o Make sure you understand what type of commitment the person desires. Some men don't want marriage, they want instant gratification. At some point, when I knew I wanted marriage, I only wanted to date men who were also marriage-minded. Why waste either of our time, right? My husband had been married before and had been divorced for nine years when I met him. So I especially had to do my due diligence because I wanted to know that he still saw marriage as a positive and viable option for him. I had to both hear him articulate that and also observe it for myself in his actions.

- **Desire to dream**—In a world full of realists, your partner should be someone you can dream aloud with. From early on, ensure that you're with someone who doesn't stifle your visions or tell you they're unrealistic. And vice versa—there's a difference between offering helpful feedback for actualizing goals and shooting someone down. Get a partner who lifts you up!

  o Take time to talk in detail about the past, present, and the future. I know couples who create vision boards together every year as a part of their New Year's tradition. It's a great way to dream together and see the goals and ambitions of the other.

The way I got to fifty items on my list is that I listed the deal breakers but also some bonuses. I often joke that my husband met forty-nine out of fifty, because he's not six foot two, so I sacrificed the four inches to date someone five foot ten! My other bonuses were along the lines of:

Likes to travel
Likes sports (even better if he's a Saints fan!)
Enjoys music and singing
Has an appreciation for Southern roots

I certainly wasn't going to walk away from a man who was so aligned with my desires but not my non-negotiables, yet so many women do. My husband had everything I wanted and listed—six foot two wasn't a non-negotiable compromise. Know the difference and keep them separate.

To complement these lists, you should also have a ***Red Flag List***.

Sometimes it takes a while to get to know people, and as you peel the layers back, you discover some things that need to be flagged. Some women see red flags and decide to wait and see just how "red" the red flag is. No. Red flags mean **STOP**. Watch your step. Do not enter. Abort mission. Because they may be on a layover to your non-negotiables. Examples:

Someone who has a history of infidelity.
Someone who can't keep a job.
Someone who can't maintain friendships.
Someone who gossips (if they're telling other people's business, they'll tell yours!).

The same red flags you ignore at the beginning of a relationship are the ones that come back to haunt you in the end. Now that you've decided on who you are, and what you want, don't turn into

Gabby Douglas bending over backward trying to make someone fit who you know in your heart doesn't. You've made a decision that this is who you are and enjoy being. Of course you'll be working on the areas that you want to improve on, but the next time you enter a relationship you will know *you* and what's important to you. That will make it easier for someone else to as well.

Fact 3: I envision my life path as . . .

Your life path is the way you envision your dreams manifesting. There will be many twists, turns, and plot twists (who'd ever think we'd see a global pandemic in 2020 and the world shut down?). You'll adjust to it all, but it's still important to know how you *want* your future to look.

Where would you want to live?
What kind of social life do you want to have?
Do you want children?
Do you plan to retire at a certain age?

Understanding these things about yourself very clearly will save you a lot of wasted time. If you live in the US and know you'll never want to move outside of the country, then don't go on vacation to Hong Kong looking for your husband. If you can't cook and hate the expectation that all women should be able to, steer clear of men with more traditional desires and expectations. Better yet, get one who knows how to cook or order out. If you know you want children, don't marry a man who has told you he doesn't. You're not in the business of changing minds.

Jeremiah, a young man I met at *Divorce Court*, grew up in foster care and never had a father figure in his life. Despite these challenges, he was an incredibly well-rounded and ambitious young man. When I met him, he had been with his wife, Sarah, for two years. He told me all the reasons that he felt he would make a great father; things he learned *not* to do by seeing what his father had done. Sarah, however, didn't want children, and Jeremiah was angry about it. The problem was: Sarah had always been upfront with Jeremiah since they'd met about not wanting children. Jeremiah married her anyway, hoping to change her mind. She didn't change her mind, and she had every right not to. Jeremiah would either have to accept Sarah for her decision or the relationship would dissolve. If having children was a non-negotiable for Jeremiah and how he envisioned his life as a family man, he'd need to find someone with the same vision.

Fact 4: I bring to my relationships . . .

Relationships are an act of service; a covenant where you ask not what your relationship/partner can do for you but what you can do for the health and success of that relationship/partner. If you want a committed relationship, be prepared to serve. Your partner should also take the same approach. Those who approach relationships trying to receive, receive, receive will end up mooching off someone else or in a relentless cycle of singledom. Make sure you know what you are bringing to the table first before you ask what someone else is contributing.

All of the reflection involved in discovering your Four Facts should give you more clarity to walk toward romance with confidence. There's no deterring a woman who knows exactly what she wants. Now it's all about how to get it. There is one more critical step in this process of self-examination: recognize that you might have to get out of your own way.

Releasing Trash Unconscious Beliefs

Oftentimes we get swept up into the drama of unconscious beliefs. These ways of thinking can be toxic and spread like a plague among women; like a bad cold virus, many of us have come down with these symptoms from time to time. The faster you get a healthier mentality and dump these trash beliefs, the quicker you are on your way to better love relationships. Maybe you've been badly hurt and as a result these beliefs are a form of self-protection. Perhaps this all boils down to your fear of getting close to someone again. It's much easier to push people away than taking a risk to open your heart again.

Sis, no one avoids getting hurt their entire lives. You have to keep reminding yourself, what's in the past needs to stay there. If you live your life based on your past, you'll bring it right into your next relationship. You'll be on high alert for any sign that a man is just like that ex who turned out to be a flake. This is not fair to him or you!

You can't be a cynic about love and attract it at the same time. Your cynicism will reveal itself in your relationships time and again until you address it. And it will show. Trust me, he will *feel* it.

It's time to do some real soul searching. If you hear yourself putting labels on men or doing any man-bashing, this is a red flag to you that you need to get past these trash beliefs. You have to do this in order to be open-minded and learn to love again.

Your fears are not serving you. They are poisoning your perspective. Take reading this book as the sign you need to garner the courage to let them go. It's really not that difficult. Just take the first step and be honest with yourself and examine your heart.

Do any of these statements sound like you?

ONE: *"All men cheat."*

Ladies, there are men out there looking for the same things you're looking for: commitment and loyalty. I can hear some women's sass responses to this already through these pages:

> Yes, but, Faith, they're harder to find than a remote control in my grandma's couch.
> Where they at, though?
> When I get one that doesn't, I will become a believer too!
> If Beyoncé can (allegedly) get cheated on, then how can I expect better?

It's hard not to get jaded sometimes when you've been betrayed or when you see it happening all around you. But what is happening in other people's relationships is really none of your concern, and you can't paint everyone you meet with the same broad brush. Just like there are a whole group of us women who can effectively communicate what we want to eat, there are men who can too. There are also a lot of men out there looking for the same things you are: loyal love. If you believe all men cheat, guess what? All the men you date will. You get what you expect and settle for.

For years, when I was dating, I used to say there was no point in getting married unless you were going to have children. Otherwise, you're just mixing your money. I was naïve then and thought that a romantic relationship was reduced to procreation and finances. When I think back on the kind of men I was dating then, they were a reflection of that mindset: career-hungry and checking life off a list but with none of the passion, kindness, attention to detail, and time spent on the little things. I had to stop thinking there were only scraps and go after that one-in-a-million, perfect man for me.

TWO: *"Of course I've got trust issues; these men have honesty issues!"*

When you've been hurt, you may fear being hurt again, and so in an act of protection you choose not to risk it. This may sound like human nature, but it's not. It means that you want to love, but at the same time you're sabotaging your relationships by pushing people away or running away before you've been hurt. In your subconscious you believe you're avoiding rejection or failure. In reality, fear won't stop you from getting hurt. It doesn't stop rejection. It won't stop betrayal. It won't stop death. What does fear stop? Life.

THREE: *"All the good ones are taken."*

You're eating at Michelin-starred restaurants, going on exotic vacations and staying in villas, securing six-figure wins at work; killing it in life but haven't manifested romantic love. It begins to feel like you're out of everyone's league and can't find a man to keep up with the lifestyle you've created for yourself. My single friends and I were all used to hearing that all the good men were taken. According to single propaganda, they were either already married, gay, or in jail. There's a huge problem with that false messaging, and if you accept that as true, then it will be true. Being pessimistic about the world around you is a surefire way to make sure you remain alone or unhappy, because only misery likes company.

First, take a deep breath and open up your heart if you've slipped into any of these ways of thinking. Don't let these unconscious biases keep you from your Forever Love.

Take some time to examine your beliefs and the messaging you've been giving to yourself and projecting to the world about relationships. See if they are aligned with what you truly want. Otherwise, you are wasting a lot of time and energy for an outcome you really don't believe is possible.

Second, stop choosing men who are in essence the same type of person who has caused you agony in the past. Don't blame a clown for being a clown. Ask yourself why you keep going to the circus.

Third, be open to love coming in a package that is different than what you envisioned. Open up your mind to who you are disqualifying, because even if someone doesn't match your preconceived notions, they could be a great fit for your life. Everything isn't so black-and-white. Give people the benefit of the doubt and evaluate case-by-case who is capable of loving you before you decide for them. Maybe you're someone who says, "I don't want to date outside of my race." Really think about why you're making these statements. Is it really about race, or is it about being with someone who values your cultural background?

Essentially, be careful who you exempt, and instead of micromanaging, look for men who complement the strengths you have. Even and especially if your strengths aren't the same, iron will sharpen iron. The right one doesn't have to be equal to you in every way. The journey you two will take will be winding. Being smart in love is not letting your intelligence, pride, stereotypes, or preconceived notions keep you from enjoying that journey.

Part II

---◦ᔐ◦---

IT TAKES TWO TO TANGO

Chapter 5

DDD: Do Due Diligence

"Who you are lasts a lifetime.
Who you pretend to be changes like the change of seasons."

—NAJWA ZEBIAN

So now you've learned some things about yourself and what you're looking for in a potential bae. You're more comfortable in your skin and ready to meet someone special. Maybe you've noticed someone who could potentially be The One—you know, the one whose photos you've been liking 2.5 seconds after he posts, hoping he'll notice and slide into your DMs. How do you apply this new, mature knowledge about yourself to meeting him? I'm more old school, personally, so I have always preferred introductions through family, friends, and colleagues—people who could vouch for the introducee. Let your close loved ones know that you are open to blind dates. Far more people are meeting these days online, through social media in particular. One of the positives of these platforms is that they do allow you to connect with a vast number of folks whose paths you may not otherwise cross. If you prefer a bit more serendipity and mystery, think about the characteristics you hope your future partner will have and frequent the sorts of places that kind of person would spend their time. For example, if you want to be with someone who appreciates art and values community, attend gallery events and volunteer for your local school's art programs. He won't fall out of the sky, so literally get out there.

I emphasize this so much, because in this digital age many rely on virtual relationships, and it can never be a true proxy for face-to-face time. Phone calls and texts are cute, but first dates are required. Don't get too wrapped up in that profile or the messages before you meet him in person. Even if you like what you see, you can tell much more about a person when you start spending time with them face-to-face. As much as we wish we could plow through the dating stage and jump right into the cuddling and power pics, dating represents a really important stage in any connection you make with another human: the "getting to know you" phase.

First dates come with a lot sometimes—discerning between red flags and early nerves…there's nothing easy about it. (*Is he Dr. Jekyll or Mr. Hyde? Don't worry, sis, people who play roles will eventually forget their lines.*) It can be even harder to get your mojo back, and feel excited to meet people after being out of the game for a while. (*Dang, he doesn't know that you prefer eating at the bar.*) Plus, these people are strangers! It would be less work to turn back around and go cuddle with your ex or an old fling, but you *must* move on! Get on with the new, even if the road ahead is unknown. As with any aspect of life, the dating phase is what we make it, and going forward I want you to change your perspective about dating. It's that simple. Think of it now as a great opportunity to let your guard down and let someone get to know the real you. Be genuine about what you really want to share with someone willing to do the same. Less superficial talk and revolving doors, more opening up and learning about each other.

If you utilized your single time to properly get in tune with your likes, dislikes, preferences, and more, then gearing up for first dates should be fairly easy for you. You worked on knowing yourself best, and you have a better idea of what you can and can't put up with in a relationship. The key is not throwing all of that out the window at the first sight of a dazzling smile or flashy résumé. Attraction is important. In fact, it's needed in order for your interest to be piqued. Just know that any guy can give you butterflies or appeal to the lustful side of you, but if you have marriage or long-term partnership on the mind, it's important to dig deeper. Remember those non-negotiables you've already laid out, because now it's time to do due diligence and get to know them. Proceed with eyes wide open.

"He's Not Six Foot Two."

Once you find someone worth talking to more than once, the dating process begins. Stop feeling the need to date. Ladies, we're no longer giving our number to the guy who we already know is a player. You know the sky is blue, so no, he cannot have your number. No, you don't want to continue any exchange with the guy who is a commitment-phobe. *("I just wanna go with the flow.")* No, you don't want to move to the next step with the workaholic who makes you want to fall asleep every time you talk to him. You know well before you hit the Olive Garden whether you're interested in him or not. The breadsticks are good but not that good. Don't drain your time or energy on things or people you're not attracted to. Many of us somehow feel sucked into a date or saying yes to giving a guy the digits just so we don't seem mean or even impolite. Women often doubt ourselves. *Maybe I'm being too picky.* You're not. Scratch all the self-doubt and believe in your truth—do you want to learn more about this person or not? No is fine, because you can go get a massage or see a movie instead.

Slutty versus Sexy

First dates are fun—butterflies in your stomach, picking out something cool to wear that says you're sexy but definitely not trying too hard—you know, the two-hour casual look.

Women get a lot of slack for what they wear on a first date. If he's disrespectful, the first thing your girlfriend says is, "What were you wearing?" Even if you had on a bikini, it doesn't warrant disrespectful comments or gestures. This balancing act between looking good and coming off cool, smart, and interesting can be overwhelming. *What do I wear that conveys interest mixed with the perfect touch of nonchalance? How can I be seductive but not slutty?* Here's my tip: throw this façade out the window. Otherwise you'll never give the people you're dating a chance to become familiar with *you.* The key is to put your best foot forward but be authentic. If you feel like showing those long, pretty legs, do it. No need to look like a nun to be treated like a queen. And the same goes if you'd rather wear your favorite hoodie. We spend so much time trying to fit a mold of who we think the cutie is looking for, rather than being ourselves and allowing that to attract our perfect match. There can be so many games being played and invisible rules that we sometimes spend more time deciphering the meaning behind it all than letting the other person get to know us. Show up to the date as *you.*

Now, in between accepting the date and the first impression is where we find a lot of potential confusion happens. As an attorney and, now, judge, I've had to master the art of asking the right questions. We're trained relentlessly on how to coax the truth out of people and read between the lines. Whether cross-examining a hostile witness or presiding over cases in my courtroom, knowing how to cut through the BS and get down to business is literally my job. So I'd like to think I know a thing or two about the talking stage and what conversations to have early on.

I've never been one for the "what's your favorite color" type questions. Snooze. And I can learn basic facts like where you work or what's your favorite color anytime, but if I'm deciding whether you are worth spending more time with, I need to know how you look at the world and what's important to you. The goal is to get to know the person beneath the surface.

I'm not a fan of grilling someone on the first date as if it's a job interview. You've heard the phrase "to the third degree" before, right? It refers to cruel and torturous interrogation tactics. Yikes, you never want that to be your impact on someone. No man wants to feel like you're crossing things off a list of qualifiers. And *you* don't want someone who just says what you want to hear in a high-pressure situation. Lower the stakes and open your ears. Getting to know someone is like dancing or dialogue: it takes two!

I always advise a coffee, lunch, or casual stroll for the first-time meet-up. You do not want to commit yourself to a three-course, two-hour dinner with someone and be stuck when you realize five minutes in he's a forty-year-old aspiring rapper. You may say, *Wow, Faith, that's harsh.* Maybe, but it's also the truth. I'm here to set you free. He's been rapping since he was thirteen, sis. At some point he had to know when to hold 'em or when to fold 'em.

Let's assume you've had a first date with someone who you think might be a good fit. Now you're at dinner, conversing over some appetizers, and homeboy has told you some really nice things about what's important to him, like how much he loves spending time with his nephews. That's great, because someone who has "a good relationship with his family" is one of your non-negotiables—based on the Four Facts. It's all going great! But wait...the entrées are coming, and you still haven't said much about yourself! Don't be so intent on assessing your date that you forget to show him who you are too and why you're worth spending time with. You want to be vulnerable and honest with people. I don't mean bawling and crying over a lobster meal about your childhood traumas or performing a monologue about your bad relationships. Just be wonderfully you. Comfortable in your own skin. True comfort with a partner comes only with time and opportunity, but don't rob your potential new boo from the chance to *actually* get to know you as opposed to the airbrushed version he's seen on Instagram (yes, you both have checked out *all* of each other's photos prior to meeting up).

Shel Silverstein, the beloved poet and children's author, wrote a poem called "Masks," which succinctly describes the danger in trying to be someone you're not, for someone you don't know, in pursuit of someone who can't be tricked. In the poem, Silverstein describes a woman and man both with blue skin who hide their blue skin from the world all the while looking for someone with blue skin. In searching for authenticity while not being true to themselves, they missed out on the joy of being with each other. Love isn't finding someone perfect but finding someone committed to seeing you for who you are and vice versa. Loving someone not in spite of but because of who they uniquely are, now that's Forever Love. If you're both hiding your true selves, how can you ever see each other?

Couth is key when making a first impression: you can be the refined diva that lives inside of you but there's a fine line between that and being someone you're not. In conversation, don't shy away from being honest and transparent in both your replies and the questions you pose.

Don't feel like you need to wait on an arbitrary dating timeline to dig a little deeper. This is the time to be intentional about asking questions that are important to you. *What are you looking for?* Basic questions that you absolutely *need* and want to be clear on before moving forward any further. If you don't fully understand his living situation, you want to get clear. If you don't comprehend his co-parenting situation, ask about it. This doesn't need to be done in an aggressive or rude way, but you should not feel afraid to ask. Many relationships are short-lived because we didn't ask the right questions upfront. You may not like all the answers that you get, but it's all good for you to know now. Imagine how much you could avoid if you know someone's true intentions from the start. A good way to learn is by asking questions and listening to the answers. Here are some ideas for good questions from your favorite judge.

1. What are you most excited about in your life right now?

This question unpacks not only what the other person values, but also lets you glance into your potential compatibility. There's no right or wrong answer, but depending on your personality, this question will take you straight to any potential personality clashes. (Like you're a business owner and they are someone who has just been thinking about it for ten years.) You can either weed them out or start a fun conversation about what the two of your visions together would look like.

2. Where do you see yourself in ten years?

This is the subtle (but actually smart!) way of asking someone if they see a serious relationship as part of their long-term plans. This is different from directly asking them if they want kids and to be married because it doesn't reduce this inquiry to being just about love. This question allows you to get a good picture of what they are envisioning for their life. If they don't mention having a romantic relationship as a goal, you can be more direct and ask them what their current relationship goals are. The reality is that you'll have a good understanding about each other's visions for your lives. Does he plan on living abroad in the near future? Or is he exploring a career path that requires long hours and other sacrifices? Perhaps he is planning to eventually move back to his hometown to be close to family. We never know someone's personal dreams, and while these dreams can change, it is helpful to know whether you're walking parallel paths early on.

3. Would you consider yourself healed from the past?

Remember, a relationship can only be as healthy as the two people who are in it. How people have dealt with their past pain is important. Unhealed trauma will continue to show up in every relationship you have until you address it. We're not responsible for the hurt others have caused, but we are responsible for our healing. This includes whether they're healed from a past breakup, abandonment, childhood trauma, work conflict, etc. You don't want to enter a relationship with someone with unprocessed pain who will project issues of the past onto you that are unrelated to you. Asking this question can help you determine if they are whole (or at least doing the work to get there) and fully ready to love.

4. *What are your religious or spiritual beliefs?*

Each person may have their own personal relationship to religion and higher powers—or none at all. I don't believe you have to 100 percent agree on everything, but it is important to know whether you can coexist, accept, and respect each other's beliefs. For me personally, I needed to be with a God-fearing man or someone who respected the fact that I'm a God-fearing woman. Perhaps for you, you don't need your partner to believe in *your* God but you do need them to believe in *something*. Or maybe it's just a nice way of getting your date talking about an area they are passionate about and learning more about what matters to them. Either way, you'll learn so much about him and yourself. If you find that the two of you have diverging beliefs, then ask (if you want children) what they plan to teach their children about their religion.

5. *What are some of your biggest fears?*

This can be as simple as a fear of heights and snakes, or as deep as commitment, fear of failure, and/or rejection. This question allows a person to understand their prospective partner's vulnerabilities, and sharing fears will strengthen the foundation of the relationship in the future. It will also help gain insight into someone's past and what helped to shape their perspective. We each have different experiences, and if we aren't aware of the fears each other has, we may unknowingly trigger them. And if you're with someone who openly mocks you during moments of vulnerability, then run, Forrest, run!

6. *Who do you look up to the most?*

Interpret it the way you want, but just know, there's a big difference between looking up to your grandfather versus looking up to Future the rapper. Whoever they look up to, this question will help you conceptualize a person's values by examining the type of people they admire and their personality type.

7. *What are the roles of a husband or wife for you?*

What can be a point of contention in a partnership is a mismatched set of expectations. Many don't realize that certain beliefs, values, and visions for our future were impressed upon us in childhood. How we watched our own parents build a life together, or not; whether we had any good examples of marriage when we were young; even what movies we watched and the media we consumed—it all shapes what we think a husband and wife are supposed to be. Asking about marriage on a first date would otherwise be a no-no, but asking about role expectations is a great way to unwind someone's mind and get a feel for how they look at the world.

8. *What are you like when you're angry? How do you handle disagreements?*

We are going to dive into this in-depth in a coming chapter, but we really saved the best for last with this one. You'll never wish you spent *more* time with an undercover hothead, I guarantee you that. You'll always be thankful for having got out of that volatile situation as fast as possible. The unpredictability and innate desire to play petty can and will come out at the times when his self-control goes out the window, and you don't want to be within a hundred feet of a man like that. Posing this question generally will first give you a feel for how your date handles conflict with others and then in romantic relationships. Pro tip: the answers shouldn't be different. A grown man who proudly gets into bar fights or road rage is bad news, period.

These questions are a good starting point for what you need to learn about someone you're pursuing, but the most important part is not to treat love like a math equation. Know your core values, but listen and allow things to develop naturally over the course of time. There's nothing worse than trying to micromanage a feeling. Let love come to you in the right time and sequence. A sign of a good date is when you can exit, not just with your crème brulée to-go box, but with a fuller sense of who you were talking to.

I recently sat down with a dear friend of mine, Caleb, who had learned this the hard way. Caleb and I have been friends for a while, and I actually attended his wedding, so his divorce eleven months later was surprising. He explained to me that his biggest mistake was not taking the time to truly know his wife before marrying her. Caleb's wedding was at a beautiful vineyard in southern California. He's a successful guitarist and music director for some of the top recording and performing artists on the planet, one of whom sang as his bride walked down the aisle! He first laid eyes on his soon-to-be-wife, Camilla, while performing. They were doing two nights near his hometown and she attended both nights, front row, with a huge smile. After the second show, Caleb went to talk to her but froze up and missed his chance. Determined to find her, he went on Instagram later that night and searched the event hashtags. He found her! After DMing, they began dating and were together for almost three years!

Now, because of Caleb's career, he was *always* on the road. So over the course of the three years, they probably spent less than six months physically together. While away, they talked on the phone, and when together it was like a honeymoon all over again. In the moment I'm sure it felt blissful, but later this would prove challenging. Caleb and Camilla had been married only three months when it felt like a switch was flipped.

She quit her job to move in with him, but he was never home. When he asked her to travel to shows with him, she said she had other plans or needed to care for her parents. Though she never seemed to have time to join him on tour, she became a huge Trump supporter, flying out for rallies and diving deep into the rabbit hole of the alt-right. Camilla also told him a month into the marriage she was "never" having children, and she had an extramarital affair six months later.

Caleb began to feel like he had been bamboozled! He explained that he didn't truly know who he married and got out of there as soon as he could. They divorced less than a year after their wedding. Caleb went into a depression but got the help he needed to push through the painful ending to his marriage. I commend his bravery and willingness to accept that the relationship wasn't going to work out instead of hanging on and delaying the inevitable. He could pay now by going through the emotional heartbreak a year in, or he could pay later when a lot more time and energy had been invested. When I asked Caleb what he would have done differently, he said he would have pressed harder to ask the uncomfortable questions and ensure the responses he was getting were true answers. This is only possible through time (do their actions reveal the truth of their words?) and in-depth dating due diligence. Attraction and physical chemistry are the floor and not the ceiling. Falling in love is easy.

Staying in love requires more—getting to know the essence of who a person is prior to a lifelong commitment is essential.

Usually after the date, as we walk or drive home, we're talking or texting with our bestie dishing it play-by-play like it was a Lakers game. But I suggest giving yourself time to reflect after each date. Sometimes we can be hyper-critical of our dates. *Gosh, he was such a wall!* Or gushing about them. *Those lips, those eyes!* Either can make us begin to create a false image of that person's personality. And we leave the date not knowing whether the person has met our standards at all. The goal is to find a judgment-free zone where you both can pull back and reflect. This will improve your dates as you go along.

Afterward, ask yourself:

1. How did I feel in his company?
2. What did I learn about him and his character?
3. What am I going to do with the information I have now?

Once you have really reflected on what you learned during your due diligence, you can better decide if you're going to forge ahead. One date can lead to investing *years* with someone, so the more you know, the better decision you can make. I went to college with John and we graduated the same year with our political science degrees. John was always a nice guy and made it clear that he was serious about marriage and finding a family. He had been on eHarmony for a couple of years, and I always thought any man who goes through that eHarmony questionnaire is definitely serious about finding love!

One night while out to dinner with friends John met Sasha— a single, thirty-five-year-old successful account executive. They exchanged contact info, and John called her the next day and asked her to dinner that weekend. As they dated, John learned that Sasha had been divorced twice and had a seven-year-old. She shared some of her past mistakes and misgivings about relationships but told John she was definitely ready and mature enough for love now. John had never been married and was a little wary, but he gave Sasha the benefit of the doubt. John listened to Sasha's explanations for the reasons for her prior divorces but never really inquired further or even talked to the mutual friends he learned they had.

They had a whirlwind romance and eloped without telling anyone six months after they met. After they got married, John started seeing another side to Sasha that began to trouble him. He witnessed her being rude to other people and found out that she had a terrible reputation among her work colleagues. Among them, she had a reputation for being disrespectful and retaliating against people she disliked.

Eventually, Sasha started to belittle *him* in front of other people, and though he tried to make it work, they divorced after a few years. One of the people John had met as his marriage started dissolving asked him, "How did you *not* know about her track record? *Everyone* knew." Ouch.

Afterward, John realized that when he married Sasha just six months after they met, he really had not done the necessary due diligence to know who she was beyond what she'd told him. He learned the *second* key to his next successful relationship would be how he would get to know them. The *first* key was patience. Sasha said all the right things, but if he had just done a bit more probing, he would have learned that her reputation had far exceeded her meeting of him. He just didn't know about it until after they had been married. To his regret.

Often we get starstruck on a date. *Oh, he plays the guitar, I love music! He's an accountant, I need someone to help me manage my money!* These are just ancillary factors. You must remember to dig deeper to find out the information that you need.

Dig a Little Deeper

I was taught early in my legal career that before you make any decision in a case, you have to do your fair share of extensive research. We are trained to read through documents meticulously and comb through supporting materials because it allows us to show up fully informed, no surprises, and ready for the task at hand. When scientists started working on the COVID-19 vaccine, there were all of these articles about the process—the research, development, testing, and protocols. In most cases the trial phase of vaccines takes years. The FDA is so meticulous because they understand the consequences if they get it wrong. They don't want to make permanent decisions on inaccurate or inadequate information. We call this due diligence, and it's something you should use when dating.

Many may joke about women turned private investigators, but fact finding is not only responsible—it's necessary. Do your research, not like a background check but a character test. No stalking necessary, but in this day and age, you should know who you're spending time with so you can break through the façade and pick up on the little cues. The key is being prepared to make a decision with your findings.

So how do you do your research without it being creepy? On dates, observe how he interacts with others. Is he an absolute gentleman to you but rude to wait staff? Was the date location thoughtful or simply flashy? Another aspect to keep track of is how he treats you. Even in the early stage there are certain telltale signs of a good man versus someone not worth your time. A man of his word will be prompt and respectful. An empathetic man and good listener won't constantly interrupt you when you speak and will ask follow-up questions instead of diverting attention back to himself.

Think about it like buying a car. When you know you're about to spend your hard-earned money, you put so much effort into evaluating whether it's a good fit, an honest sale, and worth the investment. You ask a trusted mechanic to accompany you, you look up comparative rates on Kelly Blue Book—it isn't a decision you make lightly. And even when the salesperson is laying it on thick, you check under the hood and test drive the car to be sure you didn't miss anything. Similarly, read between the lines on your first dates and make sure you leave knowing more about your date and not just having had a few laughs.

In the best-case scenario, you align well with what you find out about this person, and these truths bring you closer together. In the worst-case scenario, you find out you're not what each other is looking for. Either way, you are gifted with the opportunity to make a decision that works best for you both. I know I'd much rather know that things won't work out before becoming attached. Before you start doing each other's laundry and cooking four-course meals, make sure you know who he is and how he aligns with what you want.

So now that you have an idea of what basic questions to ask, and the guy has checked out as #Dateable, the next task is to keep the communication going as you continue to learn from each other and continue seeing each other.

WARNING: Don't feel obligated to consider a relationship locked in because he seems dateable—that's just the first step toward being with you. Your standards are high, and you're not desperate for the crumbs. You're looking for the whole pie. So you and he have to keep up the flow of communication. Some women complain that their men are bad at communication, and society has force-fed us the idea that we're superior communicators and should therefore accept the lack of it from our partners. However, when dating, that sort of thinking will send you down a bad path. We can only discover more through talking. Neither Apple nor Samsung have invented mind-reading devices.

Social Media Is Fair Game

I once turned down a date with someone based on his Instagram posts alone. A friend called me and said that a certain actor was interested in asking me out on a date and that he was a nice guy and gainfully employed. I thought, this sounds cool, so I looked at his Instagram. He was talented, had model good looks, a college degree, and a large social media following (mostly of adoring women fans). I'm sure there was no shortage of women lining up to date him. As I took a closer look at his posts, a pattern caught my attention. He posted a fair number of crude jokes and memes. In one picture there was a cartoon illustration of a woman with her legs up on a sink with a towel washing what appeared to be her private parts, and the meme read: "How women get ready when he invites you to stay over."

My friend called me back a few days later about him. "So, what do you think? Are you interested in meeting him?"

"No, it's not a good time right now," I softly declined.

I never told my friend that I had looked at his social media, because there was no need for that to get to the guy since I was no longer interested at all.

The posts bothered me, because when you're in a relationship, what your partner does publicly is also a reflection on you. I would be embarrassed if we were dating and he posted such crude jokes. To me, it spoke to his sense of humor (which wasn't a match for mine), and a high-value man simply wouldn't post a woman washing her private parts in a sink in preparation for sex. I'm not in the business of telling a thirty-eight-year-old man his jokes weren't funny (to me). I chose to believe what my eyes were telling me and turn down his dinner offer.

A person reveals tidbits of themselves on social media—in a lot of cases people only post highly filtered versions of their lives for public consumption, but what they post and share is fair game for you to look at and consider when evaluating various facets of someone's personality. Take these clues and examine them. What they find funny. What consumes their attention. What they choose to speak up about. How they interact with others.

If he's telling you he is a vegan but he's Snapchatting "Wingstop" every week, he's not being truthful or consistent. A lie is a lie.

If he's telling you he wants to settle down and be married but he's liking every thirst trap photo as fast as his little Instagram fingers will allow, then he might have a roving eye.

Listen, I'm not saying turn into *CSI* and collect a hair from his t-shirt when he's not looking to send to your in-home lab—but take advantage of all options out there for you to see what your man might be like when he's not around you, when his guard is down.

Chapter 6

Game Recognizes Game

"A woman of worth does not tolerate a complicated relationship."

—STACEY SPELLER

Less is more, single ladies. I know this can be hard to swallow for ambitious, go-getter, leave-the-games-at-the-door type of women like us. Trust me, I'm one of them. I serve the tea hot too, but stick with me for a moment as I break this down.

Repeat after me: I don't chase. I attract.

There's a lot of back-and-forth about what it means to be a twenty-first-century woman in dating and whether it's okay for women to be dominant and take charge. When it comes to dating, align with your feminist values, but leave room to be desired.

A guy friend of mine told me he took a woman to dinner once and she sent him flowers the next day. He was so confused. Men are hardwired to pursue, so a bell goes off for them when something very different is happening. And it's not a good thing.

I know you don't want to play games. I love board games—call me for a Monopoly match any day! But games in relationships? No, no, no. We don't play that. Often that's why when someone like my buddy Steve Harvey throws out advice like "less is more," meaning don't give away your heart or the cookie too soon, we become annoyed, because that sounds like a game. We don't play games, so therefore don't like the idea of being manipulative toward men. The thought of holding back just because that's some sort of dating rule sounds daunting. Now that we've gotten all that out, let's rethink this. "Less is more" simply means taking your time. You know how you break up with a guy and your mama and *all* your aunties start nagging you about slowing down and not rushing into the next one? That's what they mean. Literally observe the pace of the relationship. Set some boundaries—there is no rush. Setting boundaries is a great way to reveal a man's intentions. I don't mean micromanaging or overanalyzing. You don't want to be a goat herder. You just want to let your feminine energy allow you the space to not be moved so quickly that you don't have time to observe and learn who he is. Okay, so he's interested, but what is he interested in? Texting you until the wheels fall off, a once a month casual dinner, a relationship, or does he just want the cookie? You know how you determine that? With patience as your guiding light, it's simple: allow him to show you by his actions. Let him make his moves and you determine whether or not those moves are something you want to see more of.

When a woman pursues a man, things can go south quickly. I know it's hard because he's fine and the packaging is tight, and he's advertising all that you've been waiting for. Plus you caught a glimpse of those guns on Instagram that would be great for holding you on winter nights. I know! But stop. If you become overbearing, that will make him feel like you're trying to take him into captivity, and trust me, he will take off in flight. Or he will get so comfortable with you doing all the work, he'll get lazy! Do you want to be his Jillian Michaels or his girlfriend? Exactly.

Think of yourself as a high-value woman and act accordingly! Keisha was twenty-two years old and came into court to sue her ex, Paul, who was a serious gambler. I asked her how their relationship started, and she proceeded to explain to me that they met out one night and exchanged numbers, but Paul never called. So she called him. (SMH.)

When she called him, they set up a date that Mr. Paul never showed up for. (Surprised?) He didn't call to cancel either. He just ghosted her completely. Instead of Keisha taking that as the message it was, she decided to track him down and find him. (Why, sis?!)

She found him at a bar gambling and insisted that he take her out. Over the course of their relationship, he would continue to miss dates, leaving her high and dry, and he also started stealing from her to support his gambling habit. The sad part is by the time they showed up in my courtroom Keisha appeared to have developed a gambling problem too.

When Paul ghosted Keisha, she seemed to think that all she needed to do was work harder to whip him into shape. Meanwhile from his experience, she had set the tone from the moment they met each other that she would be the chaser and initiator in their relationship. When she tracked him down like the Hulk and demanded a date, she set the bar so low it was on the floor. Keisha got what she wanted: a relationship with Paul—who also happened to be someone who didn't value her, cherish her, or love her. What a prize. He loved himself and gambling, period. Her pursuit of him wasn't worth it.

If Keisha had known her value, she would never have gotten herself wrapped up with Paul. A high-value woman's response to a man not calling is to move on, not pursue.

That's why it is imperative that you understand how much you bring to the table. If you're thinking, *Faith, but I don't feel special. I don't feel amazing. I don't feel lovable,* sis, if you aren't there yet—and you're in the process of accepting or learning your value of being smart and sexy, loveable and kind while reading this book—then you have to fake it until you make it! Even if you don't feel it, learn to act like it, and the feelings will eventually follow. You might have to ask yourself when you're out in these dating streets WWMOD? (What would Michelle Obama do?) When Michelle was single, do you think Barack ever thought he could get away with standing her up for a date? Absolutely not. Channel your inner boss babe self and watch how everyone around you—including men—levels up to it.

The First Move

If you're getting parched and having trouble gauging his interest, there is an easy way to figure it out: wait. Wait. Wait. Wait. Don't do anything. Don't go by his apartment or his job to see what he's up to, don't start liking posts on his social media hoping he will see your name pop up in notifications and call you, don't bring him lunch. Just do absolutely nothing. That's the best thing to do! Let him be the one to reach out to you. If he doesn't call, then you'll know he's just not that interested. Men know that when dealing with a high-value woman, they should not expect her to call them. Just remember my magical word: wait. HE. WILL. CALL. YOU! If you think I'm lying, try it. Just lay low for a week. Put yourself on mute. Chill. And wait, you'll see that I'm right.

You have to let him do the work. Otherwise it sends a message to him: *I'm not used to being pursued.* It automatically diminishes your value in his eyes. You may be thinking, *What if he doesn't think I like him because I don't call him?* I'm not saying never call a love interest. I'm saying set the precedent and tone from the beginning as to what the expectations are if he wants to talk to you or see you. Your action—simply allowing him to contact you—does this. Please don't announce this as your plan—just let it be the way he sees you operate. Once you're in a relationship and things are established, call him all you want.

By the way, men love women they don't think are interested in them! You don't have to play hard to get if you are. Not hard to get as in they have to scale the castle walls and breach top-level security to get to you, but having some healthy boundaries and mystery is always an A-plus. If this scares him away or he doesn't want to put in the effort to call you, he's not ready for the relationship you want, and you'll get that message early on.

I experienced this firsthand years ago when I was attending a fundraiser. It was a who's who of Black, educated, and beautiful people, and most people seemed to know one another. So when I saw this *fine* man, I immediately asked my friend about him. She went over to him and told him she had a friend who thought he was cute and who she wanted to introduce him to. (Cue the *High School Musical* theme song.) Luckily for me he had already noticed me too, so the setup was happening. Yes, ladies, we had noticed each other from across the room! After the event, we struck up a conversation in the lobby. I found out he was an in-house general counsel at a startup company in the city and had just left one of the top law firms in New York. So here I was sending my friend over just based on how good he looked in that tux, but it turns out he was brilliant too. Jackpot. Time to update my The Knot registry! The chemistry seemed right, so when he asked for my number I just knew I was getting that phone call the next day! The next day went by, and so did the next several. Two weeks later I was sitting in my office at my law firm wondering why he never called. What in the world?! I know he thought I was cute.

He must have lost my number, I thought, trying to convince myself and heal my slightly bruised ego. What the heck, he knew what firm I worked at. He knew how to reach me. He was obviously giving me energy in the lobby; I could not miss it with all his pretty brown eye contact. I didn't get it.

About three weeks after the event, I decided to take things into my own hands. (Again? Yes, again. SMH.) I called him. "Hey, Rashad, this is Faith. Remember me? Just seeing how you're doing." I fake smiled through the phone even though he couldn't see me. He seemed pleasantly surprised, but surprised nonetheless. We spoke briefly, and he seemed genuinely happy to hear from me, but he didn't ask me out at the end of the call. I wasn't so foolish as to force myself where I wasn't wanted, and thank goodness, because I later found out why he'd never called: he had a girlfriend. At the event when he asked for my number, I think he did it as a courtesy so as not to embarrass me in front of our friends or cause an awkward moment. Bottom line is, there was a reason this man had decided not to call me. I couldn't let well enough alone and accept that reason. By me calling, it was like I was trying to convince him to change his mind. Of course that didn't work, and look what happened; that one small rejection of him not calling now turned into two. The no-calls are just as telling as the calls! Lesson learned.

In the past I used to think this sort of advice that "less is more" or to do less meant that it would seem like I was being guarded. Call it guarded or whatever you want, but you're merely looking out for your heart and protecting yourself and your time. Your presence and attention shouldn't be taken for granted. He should know that if you're taking his calls, responding to his texts, and giving him your time and attention, that means something special.

When a man values you, he will take time to plan and be consistent. These aren't archaic ideologies—these are all good, delicious things that build a strong foundation for a relationship! Letting him pursue you also allows him to express to you how he feels through his effort. That's a positive cherry on top. You'll know for sure that when you're speaking to him, he was thinking of you. Not Julie. Not Teresa. He called you.

Soft doesn't need to be weak. You can be a strong woman and still let a man take the lead. If you're someone who prides yourself on making the first move and feel like *Faith, pleeease, if I want to talk to a man, I'm picking up the phone,* and that makes you a boss or a hot girl, I suggest you check your thinking, because it actually isn't as courageous as you think. It's a higher throne to sit on believing you are worth his effort. High-value women are used to being pursued, and high-value men know that.

If you find yourself confused, because the temperature in this pursuit is sometimes hot and sometimes cold, avoid asking questions. *Well, I need to know where we stand, Faith, so I'm just going to call him up and ask him.* Sis, having to wonder where you stand with someone tells you where you stand. Someone who truly appreciates you for who you are wouldn't have you questioning your place in their life.

It can become frustrating when you don't know why there is suddenly a lack of interest. *Is it me? Is it this city? Is it my teeth? Does no one find me attractive or valuable enough as a partner?* There is so much self-doubt in putting ourselves out there romantically. I've found that books and experts rarely discuss the mentally challenging and sometimes psychologically torturous aspects of dating phases, even though that's one of the main reasons people avoid dating. It can be incredibly frustrating to know what you want (love) and feel like you're not able to make it happen.

We have to release ourselves from the "why." Ultimately, the reason he didn't call you shouldn't matter. He clearly wasn't available for you for whatever reason. Men will hit you with the "I'm just busy at work, boo" or "I have plans with some friends" and a ton of other excuses, which could all be good reasons why he hasn't called in the last few days—but weeks?! Come on, if Barack can run a country and still do date night with Michelle, we're cancelling men's excuses.

Wait for Sex... Okay, Let Me Explain

You may read this header and roll your eyes. You've heard it all before, right? That's some religious, old-school advice from my cousin Freda whose dressing is as dry as day-old biscuits but she's quick to be in everyone else's business with "It's better to marry than burn!" But none of what I'm about to tell you is to shame you; I'm telling you this because I want you to be smart when it comes to your heart. Sex and your emotions are inextricably intertwined.

Relational experts for years have told us how women bond through sex because of oxytocin, aka the Love Hormone. You've heard the stories of women who met guys they thought were average and then had sex with them, and *BOOM*. Suddenly, he's a whole snack! She sees a Barack and everyone else just sees Booker. Your body will tell you it's in love even though your brain knows *He ain't it.*

I don't know who needs to hear this, but it's not love, it's oxytocin. Don't muddy the waters and confuse the two! Sex is an emotional bonding experience, and you have to ask yourself who you're bonding to and why. So let your favorite judge make the case for waiting to have sex. Have I ever steered you wrong?

At the beginning of this book, we discussed the relational

footprints left in your life path by those you choose to unite with over time. If you agree to casual, non-committed sex with a man, what you are really telling him is: there's a low bar to gain entry into the most intimate area of your life. Let's do it, though, because our bodies want it, and the story ends there. That may work for more sexually liberated people or for fleeting moments of passion, but it rarely leads to love that lasts a lifetime.

We aren't called to be perfect, but we are called to walk in our purpose, even when it comes to sex. If penis appointments serve your purpose, then you can put this book down now and go call Booker from the barber shop. You don't need any advice for that, because sex is as common as conversation these days. To each grown woman her own. But don't conflate sex and love and think that casual hook-ups will somehow lead to a consistent and fulfilling relationship. How it starts is generally how it finishes. When you want different outcomes, do different things.

When you have decided to be intentional about manifesting your purpose partner—your Forever Love—you'll start to make different decisions about who you open up the most intimate parts of your life to. You don't need to be religious to set a standard for who can access the most sacred parts of you. Be strong enough to stand in the truth of what you really want. What is the price of admission to be in your life? Even when you show up to Six Flags they have signs at the roller coaster entrances: "You have to be 'this tall' to ride." You've paid the admission and there are even more parameters in place. No one rides for free, sis.

Many women compromise because they want this person in their life but think if sex is not a part of the equation, he'll leave. You think he won't be excited about you and will lose interest over time if you aren't doing or giving up something in order to "keep" him. If it's just sex, he's already not with you, and there's nothing to keep. This may sound harsh, but I'm on your side. Your Forever Love isn't someone who is so on the fence about you that a lack of immediate sexual gratification would turn him off enough to walk away completely. That's not the man you want to wake up to each morning, fall asleep next to each night, and build a life with to fill the in-between moments. You should take anyone who leaves your life under these circumstances as a sign that the universe is clearing out space. Sex is not a relationship. Nor will it convince a man that you'll make a great girlfriend or wife. If you're confused about where you stand, look at where you stand:

> Does he only want to Netflix and chill between the hours of eleven p.m. and three a.m.?
> Does he ever take you out on an actual date?
> Does he flake out when you two have plans outside of your apartment?

A lot of mixed messages occur when two things happen:

1. You're sleeping with him; and
2. You don't have the commitment or clarity you want.

Think back to the price of admission: ask yourself, why am I choosing this person? What is this saying about me? If you are marriage-minded, then you are seeking someone who is the same. It's a long-distance race, not a sprint. You're not dating men who are in there to smash and grab. When you make more disciplined decisions today, they pay off for you down the road.

When I was in law school, we had a final exam at the end of the semester. That one exam covered the entire course and would determine my final grade. So I asked myself: what is going to put me in the best position to achieve my goal of excelling on these exams? The people who did well on the exam were the ones who had mastered the long-distance race. They were disciplined enough to turn down parties, hangouts, Mardi Gras parades in exchange for the library because there would be a time where they would be held accountable for how they'd spent their days. Personally, I knew I would have years of my life in the future to go to every party I wanted to, but for four months prior to the test I had to buckle down. There was no cramming the night before. Discipline was the only way. I could make prudent choices every step of the way or pay later by not reaching the standards I had set for myself in the end. When you know what your end goal is, and you are focused on achieving it, every decision you make along the way should reflect that.

What are you willing to sacrifice now to get what you want later? I refused to be more discerning in my academic life than in my love life.

I can hear some responses now: *Well, Faith, why do we have to wait? Why can't we just do it when we feel like it? I'm human, and I have needs.* If we based our life choices on doing things when we felt like it, very little would get accomplished. If I went to work only when the spirit hit me, I wouldn't have a job. If I exercised only when I was motivated, I wouldn't have done a push-up since 1995. If I only paid my taxes on a whim, I would be writing this book from the state penitentiary.

The right time is not based on just feelings, it's based on a calculated decision of risk and return. You should wait until after he has demonstrated he's the high-value man you deserve and commits to the relationship. The bottom line is, time will tell. Until you have consistency, clarity, and healthy communication, say no to sex. And the reality is you can't have any of those things until you've tested them against time. Anyone can put on their Sunday best and charm you on a few dates—especially if there's something he wants. Allow time for the real him to come out, and make sure you like what you see before you surrender to an intimacy you can't take back. Be patient and let the truth reveal itself to you.

When you have a high sense of self-worth (we are all a work in progress!) you'll actually notice red flags where other people would look the other way. And you can discern red flags more when you're not falling in lust. I was listening to DeVon Franklin on Michelle Williams's podcast when he talked about the fact that most people wouldn't give a person they've known for a month the passcode to their phone, yet they don't have a problem giving them unfettered access to their body.

Often, men will tell women that they're not interested in anything serious. If he says this, believe him. He's being candid and honest with you that he wants casual sex. But instead of believing him, we women translate that as: "Oh, so I'll get him hooked and then just convince him otherwise." It rarely, if ever, happens, ladies. And then we end up heartbroken over them when in reality, it was spelled out as plain as we can see. Clarity is always a gift. Don't waste it by selectively ignoring it.

A question I get from women dating is, how do you know when it's safe to have sex with a new man? It's really about ensuring your standards for sex are aligned with your relationship goals and you're not selling yourself short. Stand in the truth of what you want in the long term. As my buddy Steve Harvey said, giving up the cookie does not mean you have a boyfriend. It just means you gave up the cookie.

You're not going to run a good man away if you set boundaries around sex. Whatever those boundaries are, the right person for you will respect and honor them. I assure you of this.

How do you set your boundaries and stick to them? First, know what your strengths and weaknesses are with men so that you aren't put into positions that constantly test your self-control. Second, know the who, what, when, where, and how of dating that works for you.

Who: Are you dating someone who respects your boundaries and isn't constantly trying to push them?

What: Are you doing quality activities on dates that put you in the best position to get to know someone? Choosing an escape room or walk in the park may be a better option for you than a late night out at your local dive bar.

When: Are your dates ending earlier or turning into three a.m. hangouts? When the clock strikes midnight and Maxwell starts playing, usually all bets are off!

Where: Are you at dinner at a restaurant or in your studio apartment?

How: Are you communicating your needs and comfort level? Always know your worth, so no one is in a position to tell you what it is and, therefore, what to do.

When I was twenty-five years old, a guy told me no man was going to date me and wait for sex until marriage. He was right in that a lot men likely wouldn't. And I remember thinking, *Wow, what if he is right.* I let that one seed discourage me for years and I made some poor decisions as a result. But in the end I realized, I wasn't interested in *a lot* of men. I was interested in the *right* one.

When you make a decision about your life it's not up to you to figure out every detail of the "how"—it's up to you to believe in it and listen to yourself. The guy telling me no one would want me was wrong.

You know yourself best. Make prudent choices that will put you in a position to succeed. Waiting for sex was a personal conviction of my husband and **me**. We waited until we were married. It worked well for us. We set clear boundaries to ensure that would be our outcome and decided that sex could wait. For one entire year from when we started dating to when we got married, we were diligent and enjoyed the ability to get to know **each other** unclouded. Kenny and I were both willing to properly place our physical desires second to the long-term goal of complete clarity as we headed toward marriage. In the end, I'm so glad we did.

Ultimately, many people use sex as a crutch or an excuse to avoid actual partnership or a distraction from the real essence of building a relationship and real intimacy. If you've ever been in or seen a friend tortured by a toxic relationship, you know that great sex was at the other end of it. People lose sight of making other forms of physical intimacy and emotional connection possible when they don't take their time. The sex isn't going anywhere, but your hearts just might if you don't set the right parameters. The exercise in restraint plus the anticipation will be incredibly sexy in its own right, trust me.

Chapter 7

When the Universe Sets You Free

"To those who have given up on love, I say trust life a little bit."

—MAYA ANGELOU

Have you ever been here? Life was coming along fine with the new bae until it wasn't. He started calling less. He showed up less. Soon he stopped showing up for you, period. You got ghosted. Let's talk about rejection. The rejection monster creeps in when you're disappointed because it doesn't work out as you expected. Whether you only went on one date or if you were right on the edge of something more, rejection can be a tough stage in your process. But, sis, it *must* happen in order for you to land on the right one.

There are different levels of disappointment or heartbreak associated with rejection, depending on how much you were invested. We're gonna talk more about breakups after long-term relationships later, but in the dating phase, get nice and comfortable with pivoting. Here's something to keep in mind on your dating journey— when people do the things they do, it's not about you. I know it's the worst cliché in the world for a disappointed heart to hear "It's not you, it's me," but when someone says it, actually believe them.

People make decisions for a whole host of reasons and mindsets that they've had long before you entered the picture. So much of what you will witness will be unhealed people's projections onto you. When you're navigating this space knowing that it's not about you all the time, it helps you not to internalize and take things personally. It hurts less. How many times have you looked back and wished you hadn't shed a single tear over that relationship that ended? You realize it was the *best* thing that could have happened. You're now doing a full-on praise dance because you realize you dodged a bullet! Cue that Yolanda Adams! We're human, so we're going to have emotional reactions—but as I like to say, separate your feelings from the facts. You don't need a happy ending before you move on—decide to move on right now in the midst of your hurt feelings. That change in perspective will change your life.

Understand that the pain you feel is temporary, and that perspective will lead you to a better future more quickly.

When I was in college, I applied for a promotion at my on-campus job—a position I thought I was a shoe-in for. I'd received positive reviews for my work, had great relationships with my colleagues, and was the most senior staffer up for the position. I was excited about the job and counting on it to help me pay for school that next year. When the decision was made, instead of promoting me, my supervisor gave the job to someone junior to me. I was so disappointed that I quit and decided to look for work elsewhere. A few weeks later, I was rejected again, this time by my peers. I'd submitted paperwork to join a sorority but didn't get the requisite votes from the members and was turned away. I remember crying on the phone to my dad late one night and telling him I now had no job and no friends! (That's what it felt like.)

Later that semester, I was walking through the student union and saw a sign for the annual Miss Louisiana Tech University pageant. The winner would receive free tuition for a year. I'd never done a pageant, but I thought: *I have nothing to lose—best case I'll win the money I need; worst case, it'll be a good distraction for a few months to take my mind off things.* But when one door closes, a window opens.

I was not going to win this pageant. That's what everyone was saying. First, there had never been a Black Miss Tech in the school's history. Second, a contestant who had already held a statewide title was also competing. I was a novice, and she was a pro! I remembered motivational speaker Les Brown once saying: "You don't have to be great to get started, but you have to get started to be great." So I decided, despite the odds, I would start preparing and put in the work (at a minimum I didn't want to be embarrassed in front of a sold-out auditorium of students and faculty!). At the end of the night, when they called out the winner, they announced my name. I won Miss Tech, which led me to Miss Louisiana, and eventually to Miss America. And in three years, I earned enough scholarships to completely pay for college and law school. More importantly, I learned how to use those platforms to give back to my community in ways I'd never imagined.

Granted, I know most people will never look to a college pageant to help finance their education, but looking at the bigger picture, here's what I realized: I would never have experienced some of the history-making moments of my life if I'd gotten the job on campus I cried over. To me, that semester of rejection was really a higher power closing doors and opening others. It turned out that I was dreaming too small. There were bigger doors to be opened ahead. From that day to this one, every time I've been tempted to get disappointed because something wasn't seemingly working out the way I wanted it to (a job, a relationship, an opportunity)—I've made sure

that my disappointment was short-lived. With patience as my guiding light, it's always worked out better for me in the long run. The
truth is, rejection is not a setback. It's a setup for you to grow, and
know that a closed door simply means something better is on the
way.

When you experience rejection—whether it's from a job or significant other—start believing that better is on the way. There's no
need to be angry when you know that better is on the way. There is
no need to be frustrated when you know better is on the way. There
is no need to suffer when you know better is on the way. When you
choose to live with this core belief, better will always be on the way.
Thanks to that summer, early on in my dating process, I realized
rejection didn't have to be a bad thing. It was required in my process.
Enter Kyle.

I was in Atlanta and met Kyle at a restaurant for dinner. In New
Orleans a couple of months prior I had met him at a Mardi Gras ball
with some friends. A friend of mine who was there thought we'd
"make a cute couple." He looked great in his tuxedo, and we had a
fun conversation for a half hour at the ball. He asked for my number
to connect afterward. He had been divorced for a few years and was
apparently ready to get back into the dating scene. He did call me
that next week and asked me out to dinner. We went to a local sea-
food place, and the conversation was nice. We had a few laughs. He
was a nice guy, but there were no sparks. He didn't do anything that
raised any flags for me, but I didn't really feel a connection.

Unfortunately, he asked me out again. Unfortunately, I said yes.
(Sigh.) I don't know why I said yes. Even though he didn't give me
butterflies, I guess I decided to follow through and see if the second
date would be different.

Do you believe that for our second date he stood me up? Momen-
tarily, I was in disbelief and offended. Surely, Mercury must be

retrograde. I checked the calendar. Nope. I was just plain ole stood up. How rude of him not to keep his word or at least let me know he wouldn't be able to make it! Another hour passed, and I reached my max. I was more than frustrated now. How could he stand me up?? I barely even liked this guy, and yet he had made me look like the loser! Something about me getting worked up over a man I knew I didn't want began to feel silly to me. I could internalize this and think less of myself, or I could silently thank him for giving me an out from this date. Instead of sending off a bunch of texts calling him everything but a child of God, I put my phone down and thought for a second. Why should I let him make me feel rejected? The answer was that I didn't have to. I then just chalked it up to a life lesson and moved on. I went to dinner with my girls instead and had a ball.

I never reached out to him. We never communicated again. I had been ghosted. Ghosting can trigger unhealed emotional or physical abandonment wounds. This time I took the ghosting well, but in the past, like many women, it made me question myself: "Am I not good enough, unworthy, or somehow undeserving?"

The truth is his decision to stand me up said everything about him and nothing about me. It spoke to his character and integrity, not mine. My ego was bruised a bit, but the bottom line was it was great to find out so early on in the "getting to know you" stage that he was a schmuck. No time wasted. I kept it moving.

I did have a couple of daydreams about channeling my inner Julia Roberts in *Pretty Woman*. I envisioned running into him randomly at some event looking fabulous and saying, "Remember me?" Big mistake!" But he wasn't even worth trying to prove anything to. Sometimes you just gotta shake the dust off your feet, announce "Next!" and move on.

(PS: He's still single . . . to no one's surprise.)

Rejection Is Redirection: The Best R & R

If you're on the receiving end of rejection in dating, here's what I want you to understand: the doors aren't closed, they are revolving. Internalizing rejection from the men you meet will drag you down, ladies. Don't let it mean anything more to you than what it was. Maybe someone on Hinge swipes right, but then they drop off from responding to your messages. Oh, well, that's just what happened, end of story. It doesn't mean anything about your profile pics or that you were coming off as desperate in your responses. No, let's not think so deeply about it. Homeboy just never responded, and now it's on to the next! Maybe after a few dates, he declared his feelings for you, but next week he posts a photo to Instagram with another woman. It's a mistake to question your self-worth based on his actions. Don't give your power away so easily. You'll be all over the place emotionally giving your power to every Tom, Dick, and Davon you meet. And many times it's just not that deep as to why they rejected you. And being rejected by a guy who does that is a gift—good human beings aren't cavalier with other people's feelings. Wish the new girl well.

One night in college I went to an event called Casino Night. Everyone dressed up in formal clothes and played casino games to win prizes at the end of the night. I decided to ask a guy named Jesse to attend the event with me. Jesse reminded me of the actor from *Grey's Anatomy*—Jesse Williams. He had green eyes and a short, curly haircut. Everyone we knew called him "pretty boy." He took it as a compliment and would often smile back wryly at the girls who stared at him as he walked by. We were friendly enough, and I heard he was single. I saw him one day, walked over, and very casually asked him if he'd go to the event with me. He got a little flustered and fumbled over his words a bit. And then he told me no. He didn't really give a reason, and I stood there embarrassed. Rejected.

My ego was bruised, but I picked up my confidence enough to show up to Casino Night in a long, black sequined dress. I felt like a queen that night. My sparkly dress felt more exciting than any date could. After that I would rarely see Jesse around, if at all. Five years later, I was shopping with some friends in a local mall, and I ran into him. I had forgotten all about Casino Night. We had both graduated and were having a nice exchange catching up on our new adult lives as my friends stood looking. He was still good-looking. As I was about to walk away, he asked if he could talk to me alone. I was doubly shocked when he said, "Do you remember when you asked me to go to Casino Night years ago?" I thought, not really. "Well, I told you I couldn't go with you, but it wasn't because I didn't want to. I wanted to go, but I didn't have a suit, or any money to get a suit, and I was too embarrassed to tell you."

Well, don't that beat all. I thought for sure every guy had at least one of those oversize Steve Harvey suits in their wardrobe repertoire. Not Jesse. My heart immediately went out to him. And I also thought back to myself and how my feelings had been hurt at the time.

We often take rejection personally. We go down a rabbit hole. Am I pretty enough? Smart enough? Successful enough? I could have made up an entire story in my head about why Jesse didn't want to go out with me, about my worth as a woman and as a person, when it was really about this guy not having a suit to wear to the event.

Singlehood can look like a string of rejections, if you let it. However, those rejections are simply redirections. And that's exactly how we should look at them. Instead of making sweeping generalizations about ourselves or becoming angry, be thankful that your journey is directing you to a different path. The human mind, body, and soul are designed and equipped to bounce back from anything that comes our way that is harmful. But just because we are resilient doesn't mean we should play Russian roulette. Accept life's redirections, because some of them are saving you.

I had a pretty serious experience with this a while back when I accepted a dinner invitation from someone with a high-profile position. Let's call him Jadon. Jadon was everything a girl from Louisiana could hope her soon-to-be bae would be. He was not only a gorgeous man, but he was incredibly accomplished. It's rare to be that kind of total package. I was actually a little intimidated about the dinner because I was thinking that he could go out with any celebrity, actress, or model. I wasn't any of those things. We had a great conversation, and Jadon was a nice piece of arm candy as well as a smart guy to talk to. I was living in New York, and he was based in another state—we planned to see each other again, but eventually things started wearing thin when our schedules didn't match up. Once I realized that it wasn't going to work out, I felt really disappointed. I knew I was going to be fine, but I did have a night out and dinner with one of my girlfriends to lament, "I finally met someone I actually like, and, again, for whatever reason, it fizzled out." Dang.

A few weeks later I saw him on television, but not for his expertise in his field—for raping several women! Jadon was being arrested for allegedly meeting women at bars and clubs, taking them back to his apartment, drugging them, and raping them. Not only that, but one of the alleged incidents took place two days before our dinner date! Whoa, Nelly!

I was shook. I literally walked around in a daze that day. What kind of bullet had I just dodged? Never in a million years would I have thought he was capable of such a thing. I thank the good Lord for protecting me from a situation I didn't even know was dangerous. I share this to say, you don't need to know the *why* every time something goes in a different direction than what you planned. You don't need to head to the group chat for a play-by-play breakdown and analysis every time someone exits your life. Just let it go. I know people like to say that "everything happens for a reason," and when no one can tell you the reason, the cliché starts to feel like an empty promise. Sometimes you just have to trust the process and know the outcome will reveal itself eventually. And when it does, you will understand. Not all that glitters is a diamond. If it's for you, it's for you.

As I navigated the dating space, it felt more like "self-protecting." There was a lot of mess out there that I did not want to be involved in. Single women have a lot to deal with. Have you ever met a guy who seems normal? I mean someone you met grocery shopping, which is a very normal activity. You exchange numbers, and before you get in your car there's a pic in your phone that isn't quite an eggplant. Gross, right? But stuff like this happens to single women *all the time*. It's probably one of the reasons why you are looking for a high-value, good man—so you don't have to deal with the craziness.

Then, it can be so disappointing when you finally think that you've landed Mr. Right and he turns out to be Mr. All Wrong. He lined up pretty well with what you thought you were looking for: just a plain ole good, intelligent man of God. Or so you thought. Until you discover that wandering eye or his sweet tooth as a serial dater. And when you ask about it, he has the nerve to tell you, "Let he who has not sinned cast the first stone." (Cast him out and run, sis.)

The point is, don't go crying over spilled milk when you know there is a fresh carton waiting for you. Anyone you didn't end up with simply wasn't for you. And not only will you be better for growing through these relational challenges, but as you continue to live your high-value life, they'll often be the ones pining. (I can't tell you how many times someone I've dated from the past has ended up in my DMs to "just say hello.") High-value people don't miss out, because they know divine timing is perfect. It's everyone else who should be mourning the loss of *you*. Have this mentality in your dating life and it will change everything. In the end you will save yourself a lot of tears and about five pounds from that ice cream you're not going to consume, because you've realized that you should be rejoicing when Mr. Wrong has gotten out of your way, and everything is lining up to work out for your benefit.

Chapter 8

Committed to What?

"Love has nothing to do with what you are expecting to get—only with what you are expecting to give—which is everything."

—KATHARINE HEPBURN

So let's talk about when things are working out. You've met someone you like, and it's going well. What does commitment look like to you? To him? Are you both committed to the same things? By that I mean, how does each person define commitment? Is it reduced to fidelity, or do you require more? What is your covenant with this person going to be?

On *Divorce Court*, I often see two things: couples who have different definitions of commitment and couples who have not done the work to prepare themselves for commitment. First, in disputes where couples have different definitions of commitment—for example, he doesn't see texting as cheating, but his partner clearly feels differently—the lack of clarity causes *huge* problems. You don't want this to be the direction your relationship goes in. Especially with two people who are both strong in their beliefs, you can find yourselves moving fast in opposite directions, and the distance created can feel hard to come back from. Early conversations about commitment will lead to clarity, and the vulnerability will lead to a new level of intimacy that can make both parties feel safer in the relationship.

Second, it's easy to fall in love, but it takes work to stay there. As we discussed in chapter 4, commitment must be sustained; it's not a one-off event but a daily act. During the honeymoon stage, we often start to get comfortable and forget that a real, loving relationship will require a lot of effort, compromise, sacrifice, and service. A relationship bears as much fruit as you are willing to grow, so don't run from the work chasing after the fun parts. In committing to this man, also make a commitment to yourself to show up fully and be self-aware enough to know that you still have things to learn in order to stay on the right track. You don't make an expensive investment and then ignore its maintenance needs. On the contrary, you become even more vigilant about what is required to grow that investment tenfold.

Level Up

In the early stages of a relationship, many women get caught up in the romance. It definitely feels *oh, so good* to be wined and dined by someone who appreciates you. After many, many nights and holidays solo, it can feel especially nice to have those flowers delivered on Valentine's Day or the surprise romantic getaway, but don't confuse those for the only perks or objectives in a relationship. When you talk to couples who have been married for twenty-five-plus years, they don't mention the gifts or the superficial things they've gained. They say things like "she makes me a better man" or "he pushes me and is my biggest cheerleader." The true tell of a solid relationship is how much you both grow.

Relationships present us with tremendous opportunities to evolve and expand. If we go into relationships looking at what we can put in them versus what we can get out of them, they will transform us. Iron sharpens iron, and the beauty in committing to someone who inspires you is that they lovingly push you to level up. And this level up will not only benefit the love you two share but also spill into your professional life, your non-romantic relationships, and your overall character.

When you're in a committed relationship, expect a tremendous amount of growth. Like working out a muscle, each time you stretch and flex it, you're made better for it. Here are a few of the areas you can expect to grow in.

Patience

We all know that people can get on our absolute *last* nerve. That much you can't control. But how we respond to it is a direct reflection of who *you* are and will impact the longevity of your relationship. A good relationship requires strong communication and patience. If you can master this with your man, it will serve you well not just with him but in your career, with children (yours or others'), and in your day-to-day life. Sometimes you have to ask yourself: is this really a big deal? The question serves as a reality check and causes you to immediately become more reflective and increase your level of perspective. What you were once ready to make into a mountain now becomes an "oh well." You'll find that ocassionally forgetting to do a task like taking out the trash or picking up your soy latte on the way home like he promised aren't big deals. Many single women think that patience is something other women in relationships are magically born with—it's not. It's a muscle that just gets stronger with time. Don't worry, you may get hot right now thinking about your latte being forgotten, but you'll get better.

Acceptance

The powerful thing about grace and acceptance is that when you learn to extend it deeply to others, you can do the same for yourself. Finding someone who loves you, flaws and all, will push you to honor your own imperfections and accept those in others. At the heart of every friendship, romantic relationship, and marriage is acceptance of the fact that we are human beings doing the best we can. This sounds so obvious, yet many couples forget about this little fact about life. How many of us treat strangers we encounter on the street better than we do our own partners? We show our bosses more respect than we do our significant others. That's what the phrase "I'm only human" means. By virtue of who we are, we'll make mistakes. We change. We change our minds. We grow. We use good judgment—and sometimes we don't. We get depressed. We feel insecure. We don't always listen. We have doubts. We have fears. When you're in a love relationship, it's easy to forget you're not perfect *and* you're also not with a perfect person. Sometimes people will let you down. There's something remarkable about seeing your partner as a human being instead of demanding something from them that isn't realistic: perfection. I'm not suggesting that you put up with affairs or other destructive behavior—I'm suggesting that you always allow your person the space to err. To err is human, to love is divine.

Compromise

The inability to compromise sinks relationships faster than icebergs sank the *Titanic*! You can't come into a union expecting to run the whole show and always have things your way. Not only is it unrealistic, but you might as well just remain alone if that's your desire. Your partner comes into the relationship with different experiences and perspectives, and appreciating the differences and compromising is what makes it all work. Life is really about compromise. Dozens of times every day things can go wrong or turn in a different direction than you would like. These moments present us with choices on how to respond or react, and I suggest that you choose peace over frustration. This doesn't mean you're condoning and/or looking past bad behavior. It's choosing to help keep the peace. There's no question that when you and your love partner make this choice often together, your relationship will benefit greatly. We'll discuss this more below.

Stronger Together

When you're on a team and one of the members hits a home run, scores, and wins the game, the entire team wins. *Everyone* wins. The same should be true for committed relationships. Are you whole enough to be committed to the other's success? Or will your ego and pride keep you from building your significant other up?

Here's how I learned that finding someone who wanted to be a partner was more important than finding someone who wanted to be a lover.

Several years ago I received an interview request from *Essence* magazine to profile my show at the time, *Judge Faith*. I was very excited because I've always loved *Essence* and would often collect the beautiful covers and incorporate their fashion and makeup advice into my own arsenal. As soon as they asked to cover me in their next magazine issue, everything became about preparing for my photo shoot. I was as eager as a kid going to a playground! It was such a huge milestone for me to have a publication by and for Black women highlighting my work! I immediately went to share the news with this guy Daniel I'd started dating. And the look on his face said it all. Flat. Blank. Nothing.

I repeated, "*Essence*!" Just in case he didn't hear me. Maybe he didn't hear me. Or maybe he was in shock that he was graced with the presence of a soon-to-be *Essence* feature queen! But as the silent minutes crept by, I realized that instead of being genuinely happy, he actually looked more concerned. Then he looked embarrassed or something. It was written all over his face! He wasn't genuinely happy for me. He said the right words: "Congratulations." "I'm so happy for you." But his expression, tone, and energy was more *She's moving ahead faster in her career than I am in mine.* He felt threatened by the higher profile he saw me achieving. He knew how much my professional growth mattered to me, and yet he couldn't bring himself to celebrate the moment. I knew I couldn't be with him. He couldn't be on my team. If he couldn't celebrate my success with me, I'd have to let him go. Never settle for a man you have to dim your light to be around.

Michelle Obama talked about her marriage at the 2019 Essence Fest. She said when you choose a husband, you are choosing a teammate. This resonated so much with me, because I've always likened finding a husband to selecting co-counsel. When you're an attorney, everyone thinks you do it alone, but it all really boils down to who you want in your corner when the stakes are high. This may be abstract for some of you, but really think about it: you have to trust that your partner will have your back, whether catching things you couldn't or filing paperwork late at night. In love, the stakes are even higher, because you're playing with each other's hearts; knowing you have a teammate who will both celebrate your highs and fill in when you're low is critical. At the end of the day our collective priority is the same: the client we represent. In love, you have to *know* that you're in this together. That support shouldn't be conditioned on whether things are also going well for you; not showing up for your partner is definitely a problem.

As a hardworking and successful woman, I've had to be vigilant about avoiding men who weren't ready for a woman who doesn't play small. Some men are attracted to an independent woman, and some are fearful that independence threatens their place in your life. Unbeknownst to me, the man I was dating was fearful of me leaving him or that I'd feel like I was better than him. That couldn't have been further from the truth, because he was successful himself. I was proud to be by his side, but it was becoming clear that he couldn't see through the fog of his own self-doubt. Soon, he began flirting with other girls and acting out on social media because that was where he was more comfortable and "safe." Instead of waiting for me to walk away from the relationship, he pushed me away first.

I had no interest in nursing the ego of someone who couldn't handle even a magazine article about me, especially when I had never thrown my success in his face. This signaled to me that he wasn't able to see the value in *us* beyond having a woman behind him, building him up, and that wasn't the relationship I wanted. And if he couldn't be happy for me or handle me when I was winning in one article, I knew he couldn't handle where I was headed. And that's exactly what happened—he's not in the picture, and my career is reflective of Maya Angelou's words: *And still I rise.*

Communication

When you're committed to growing together, you learn how to respond to other people on a level that elevates them and your relationship. You learn to become more skilled in finding the words to communicate that will enhance your foundation instead of breaking it down. You learn the value of listening not with the intent to reply but with the intent to understand. It's all a reflection of how much you care and how much time and energy you're willing to invest to ensure your partner feels good in your presence. In chapter 10, we'll talk more about this and how to navigate conflict in a way that doesn't let you lose sight of loving communication.

Perfect relationship dynamics aren't real. Strong relationship dynamics are built and maintained. It's like wine: it gets finer with time and investment. All of these newfound characteristics that you'll gain from a relationship don't happen overnight. It's fake news if someone in a relationship tells you that she learned patience, acceptance, and communication in a week with her new man. There will always be challenges and transformations needed when growing into a partnership with someone else—whether a business partner or a boo. This is especially true for strong, high-value women who have been making it on their own. Once the honeymoon phase is over, they can easily skirt out the back door for a glass of Prosecco instead of doing the work. But if the person you've found is worth it, then keep at it; you have the opportunity for a long-term lover. The key is a mindset that understands that a healthy relationship is a daily practice.

Strong, Independent Women . . . and the Men Who Love Them

Let's get 100 percent clear on something—secure men are not intimidated by women with their business together. There is no reason to dim your light, and as smart, high-value women, we won't be putting down our cape for a relationship. As queens, we won't be taking off our crowns. As lady bosses, there won't be any stepping back. There's no need to present a false narrative to ourselves or significant others for the sake of a relationship. We're built strong and independent for a reason—it's how we accomplish all the great things that we do—and we love ourselves for it. With that said, let's discuss how we transition from high-value, strong single women to high-value, strong women in healthy relationships. It's not always an easy transition; it can be a tricky dynamic because, remember, we're pretty mighty! First, we need to be with a man who is totally secure with an independent woman and won't need to be coddled or constantly reassured. When you're talking to a man who wants to commit to an independent woman—is he okay with you spending time away from him alone? Is he okay with the money you make? Is he able to dream with you? What are his expectations about each of your roles in the relationship? Is he comfortable allowing the spotlight to remain on someone else?

Independence has been incredibly important to me as a career-focused, working woman. Some people worry that independence keeps men away, but it only keeps the right ones away—the weaklings who *should* stay far the heck away from you!

Dump the wing clippers as soon as they come creeping about with their little scissors; cutting down who you are, what you do, what you want, how you want to love, etc. You know the types: you say that you'd like to one day move to a certain neighborhood, and they roll their eyes and call you bougie. Or you say, "Boo, I want to visit the pyramids," and certain other classy travel destinations on your bucket list, and all they say is, "You need to be satisfied with what you got right here." Clip clip, chip chip, they go. Sometimes they love you and they don't mean to do this. It's just that, unfortunately, even when two people may be on the same page, external factors can contribute to someone feeling inadequate. People have so many opinions and often project them on you. It says nothing about you and everything about them. If you're not careful, other people's viewpoints can shape the way you approach your relationship.

Shortly after I got engaged to my now husband, Kenny, he was inducted into Prince George's County Public School Hall of Fame. That night I sat at the table with him alongside other honorees like six-time world champion boxer Sugar Ray Leonard. It was a magical night, and watching Kenny be celebrated made my heart swell. During the evening, a woman came up to me and said, "I just want you to know even though he's getting all the attention tonight, you're amazing too." She meant well, but for the life of me I couldn't understand what would cause her to believe I somehow needed some reassurance.

Later in the evening, another woman said something similar: "I know everyone's here for Kenny, but you're great too." Here I was happily supporting my man and fine not being in the spotlight. I was reveling in his success, but for some reason people thought I'd feel less than and wanted to "reassure" me. My love and admiration for Kenny were unwavering, yet unintentionally people thought otherwise. Thank God, the ground of our relationship didn't cultivate and nurse those seeds, but you'd be surprised how many people become undone by comments like that.

There should be no question of who your biggest fan is and,

thankfully, it's always been that way with Kenny and me. We've both experienced ebbs and flows in our careers, and through it all there's never been one hint of jealousy or insecurity. Why? Because when you're on the same team, a win for one is a win for both. You should never fear basking in your greatness. A strong man will only help you grow, not stunt you.

Becoming a united team is the goal. Relationships are beautiful when two people move in the same direction and are in sync. Supporting each other's goals, serving as a sounding board, sharing a life together. But those pros don't come without challenges. The sacrifice is checking your ego at the door too and being willing to open yourself up. As independent women who are secure, we know that there's a difference between staying authentic and letting pride—or fear—keep us from a beautiful partnership. In order for us to handle the transition from numero uno into a killer duo, one with our committed partners, we must identify the target of our challenges and kill it: our egos. Stomp it out like your favorite NWA theme song would have you do. This is what we call the ego death—when you let go of needing to do it all alone or needing to control every aspect of life.

It may be tough to identify the parts of your ego that need to be put in check. After all, they probably have been very beneficial in other areas of your life like your career, or being a lead caretaker for your family members, or even in parenting, but you know when these qualities are a problem in your relationship house when you've heard it over and over again from people who love you. If this discussion about ego holding you back creates even a little tinkle or trigger of emotion stirred up, then I suggest you address it. Ego death creates space for vulnerability, trust, and consistent communication. In being vulnerable we give our partners permission to do the same and trade playing games for building a winning team. You've already confirmed that your values are aligned, so submit yourself to your partner and ask that he do the same with you.

We all have egos. Ego is a person's sense of self-importance, but when you're becoming a team, there's no room for putting *me* above *we*. A healthy relationship can't let egos rule the day. To build a partnership rooted in patience, acceptance, and compromise, selflessness is necessary. The definition of *we* as a verb is "to combine two factors or qualities, especially desirable ones." If you are too busy keeping a wall up around your heart and all the beautiful things you bring to the world, you'll miss out on seeing his. Many women I know who are brilliant and no-nonsense in careers push great men away simply because they couldn't commit to becoming one with each other.

Ego tells you that you don't "have" to do something for your man. Love reminds you that you *want* to do things for someone you care for. Ego tells you that you don't "owe" him an explanation. Love reminds you that you have nothing to hide from someone you trust. Ego tells you that you always have to have a backup plan. Love reminds you that if you give it your all, you'll never wonder if it was you that didn't try hard enough. By being smart in dating, you've already filtered out men who weren't good for you. Now is the time to be committed to not letting past experiences keep you from giving the next guy a fair chance to be exactly what you were looking for.

Who Wears the Pants?

In the context of your committed relationship, it's important to understand the power of your partnership. Often people who find themselves incapable of maintaining a relationship feel that sharing a life and compromise has to mean conceding, or giving up things that are important to them. We've all heard the jokes men make about marriage and committed relationships feeling like a ball and chain or the end of their freedom. Women also worry that marriage is where independence goes to die. While these jokes have pervaded the way some approach love, they couldn't be further from the truth.

The relationship that I want you to have doesn't hold you back or down; it frees you even more and empowers you to show up every day as your best self. This is possible, knowing that no matter what there is at least one person, your bae, who is rooting for you and actively supporting you. Now that you have a partner, step into your collective power and commit to do new things to nurture and maintain that relationship. When you work hard, you get to play even harder, right? Relationships are no different. When you put in the time early on in a relationship to learn your partner, show them the real you, and create healthy boundaries, you will have a stronger partnership down the line. One with more ease and emotional safety. You'll have a solid foundation to stand on. Everyone wants their rock in love, and this is how you get it: commitment.

Commitment is not about submitting so much that you lose what makes you *you*. You are not giving up power, you are expanding it. The power in any successful couple is in the willingness to be two individuals moving toward goals with each other. Instead of power tripping and trying to assert authority all the time, try giving a lot and taking a little. A commitment to being better is only possible when you both see the relationship as an opportunity as opposed to preparing for worst-case scenarios. Here are the three types of power in relationships that make (*or break*) the commitment and partnership stronger.

1. **The Power of Words**—Be intentional with your words because they can shape what happens in your love life. We all have that story from childhood—a small comment from a teacher or insult from a peer that we may still battle to this day.

Even though we know the person couldn't have known their words would stick with you throughout life, they did! A person's intentions don't change the impact of their words. Harsh communication feels harsh, even if you meant to be helpful. Love is often received with love. If you want to be cherished, then cherish your man by not hitting below the belt and saying things that will hurt him and, at the same time, both of you.

2. **The Power of Respect**—Become the loving person you seek. This should be intuitive, and yet we often are careless with our partners, forgetting the Golden Rule: do unto others as you would have them do unto you. Offer your partner the kind of love that you want to receive from them. Put yourself in their shoes, and often! Would you date you if you were of the opposite sex? Would you be fulfilled by the love you give others?

3. **The Power of Kindness**—Nothing kills romance in a relationship faster than unkindness. You can have a lot of things going on, but when you can be kind to a person in the midst of it, it can defuse a lot. Especially under quarantine, you can learn this quickly. It's easy to wake up on the wrong side of the bed and treat the people around you like a punching bag. A commitment to simply being kind goes a long way. I never wanted to tolerate my partner or, worse, to be the couple that fights like cats and dogs. Choosing kindness has been a saving grace.

These are the small actions that demonstrate how committed you are. So many people think they are such a prize because the bills are paid and they don't cheat. There is *so* much more to being someone's partner that will require checking your ego at the door and being a person of your word if you want to take wedding vows with you. A marriage is the most important contract you'll ever enter into, and it will require you put your best foot forward in every way.

Chapter 9

Love, Actually

"We are told that people stay in love because of chemistry, or because they remain intrigued with each other, because of many kindnesses, because of luck. But part of it has got to be forgiveness and gratefulness."

—ELLEN GOODMAN

Okay, I'm just gonna say it: Forever Love feels soooooo good! I feel like I've been sharing a lot of warning signs, because there's plenty of that needed. But at the end of the dark tunnel is a love so sweet the honeybees want the recipe. So deep, the ocean is taking notes. So honest, it will make a priest draw closer to God. So strong, it puts Gorilla Glue to shame.

I know we've each learned in one way or another that not everything that glitters is gold when it comes to finding a good man, but when you *do*, embrace it. It's a thrilling feeling to find someone who makes you laugh, asks good questions, and shows he cares. To fall in love feels so sudden, it's like an exciting rush of emotion that you had no idea was inside of you suddenly has rushed to the surface like some sort of tsunami in your soul. Finding someone who sees you in all your beauty and brilliance, and makes you feel as special as you know yourself to be, feels hands-down amazing! While falling in love feels good, beware of equating this with love, actually. Love, actually isn't a rush despite what many of the people who come to *Divorce Court* might believe and those in Hollywood try to drill into us.

Take Sharon and Keith, who met at a Beyoncé concert, so sparks were already flying! The attraction was immediate; as Yoncé sang "All the Single Ladies," they chatted the night away together at the bar. As the curtain dropped, Keith asked Sharon out for a date the following night, and she happily agreed. Keith was fun and an outgoing guy, just her type! She was excited. Sharon left the concert doing all Beyoncé's signature moves due to meeting this potential new boo, but her girlfriend quickly cautioned her about Keith. "He used to date someone I know. He's a serial dater, and he moves quickly from one woman to the next and has quite the reputation of coming on strong and leaving just as abruptly." Sharon thanked her friend for the concern but continued to skip along to her own beat. Keith was all that, and her friend was not going to block her blessing! By the end of the first date Keith looked deeply into her with his brown bedroom eyes and said, "You are the woman I've been looking for my entire life." Sharon nearly melted. She also immediately deleted "Single Ladies" from her playlist. She was so caught up in his words that she ignored a little voice in her head that kept repeating, *Girl, slow this guy down.* The voice was nagging her to take more time to get to know Keith better before allowing him to move things so fast. But the whirlwind romance knocked sis right off her feet. She had been waiting for someone like Keith for so long that she didn't want to apply the brakes and mess this good thing up.

Keith asked Sharon to be his girlfriend a week after they met. To

Sharon, Keith fit all the surface requirements for a perfect husband: handsome, ambitious, successful, high-profile job, Christian. She figured she'd deal with everything else in time, as they got to know each other.

But that never happened. As time passed, she never really learned much about Keith. After many months, she learned nothing more than what she had in the first few weeks. He was unwilling to open up and would deflect questions about his life—his goals, dreams, ambitions, or his past. He wouldn't get into deeper conversations about anything. Keith finally lived up to his reputation and broke things off with Sharon abruptly over the phone. She never heard from him again. Devastating.

It took several months, a few good cries, and some nights out with her girlfriends for Sharon to see that she never knew Keith and never should have jumped into a relationship with him after a week. She was so swept up with the idea of love that she didn't take the time to get to know Keith before moving so quickly. There was no proper foundation built between them, and in hindsight she saw how her rose-colored glasses had led her to be impatient with foundation building, and that misstep had set her up for heartbreak. Your desire to be in love must take a back seat to your desire to be in love with the right person. One must walk into love, not fall.

True love is built on the foundation of a strong, intimate bond that can only be formed through time and experience. Imagine you've been told you can have your dream house in record time, but if it's built on sand, how long will it last? How well would you sleep at night with a storm raging around your house? You'd be left sleeping on the street, girl! It is the same with relationships. Think of your relationship as the house and your love as the foundation. You have to nurture that love and build on it so that it can be secure enough to sustain you through life's stormy times. Keith was a serial dater, but maybe things would have gone differently if Sharon had not let him put her heart in the sand.

The New Rules for Love

What is true love? It depends on who you ask. Some people equate love with chaos, depending on what they grew up around and how they saw love being defined. For them, love was someone not showing up, not being dependable, experiencing addictions, and having screaming matches, so love took on a toxic meaning. But it was their norm. And then there's the flip side where we're exposed to fairy tales and Disney movies and don't even mention how we all ugly-cried watching *The Notebook* or cheered on Stella getting her groove back. Bottom line is, love has been highly romanticized by Hollywood, and it's often to our detriment.

I often ask the couples who come before me on *Divorce Court* how they define love. I've heard a variety of descriptions:

"Love is powerful." "Love conquers all." "Love wins." "Love will save the day." We all learn about love from these types of psychological and social frames and references. From the moment we begin ingesting media (whether through magazines, ads, film, or music), we are fed visions of love on our digital screens that love is exciting and thrilling and easy. It looks as if love just works itself out on its own. That's why as we get older and haven't gotten that love diamond that society has taught us must be our expectation, we're confused. We then spend a lot of energy on getting it...or sex. But there's no Wiz behind a smoke screen orchestrating love. Finding and keeping love is rarely as easy as slipping and falling into it.

The Truth about Love

In reality, love has romance, butterflies, and euphoric moments, but it also has challenges and conflict. Love encompasses service, sacrifice, and honest and healthy communication. And so it's about balancing it all in a healthy and emotionally mature way. This is why marriage counseling comes so highly recommended—which I'm going to dive into even more deeply later on. You should enter a relationship having talked to each other and addressed those elephants in the room you've been hoping would sort themselves out. Two people have to understand that a lot of love is about service.

I recently attended a friend's gorgeous wedding in the hills of Washington state. The ceremony was magical, and no detail was spared in the décor, yet they were divorced in less than a year. My friend Jose, the groom, knew all along he didn't want to be married but went through with it because he had already acquiesced in proposing. In Jose's head, it was too late, and he didn't want to rock the boat with so many people excited about their wedding. In my opinion, inviting all of your loved ones to this huge celebration and then having to break the news that you didn't last even a year is more devastating than calling off an engagement.

I can't know all that was going on between those two, but I'm sure his bride would have preferred honesty up front. As the saying goes: it's never the lie that gets you. It's the cover-up that makes things far worse. The point is, love someone enough to be transparent about your concerns so that you can make decisions as a team. Maybe Jose and his partner had already paid the deposits, but there was always the opportunity to move the wedding back to give himself more time to revisit the best course of action as opposed to letting it just happen for appearance's sake. He may have thought he was saving face by giving her that dream wedding (oh, please), but I'm sure it only hurt more to have all those memories cancelled a year later!

It's time that we redefine our definition of love so that our relationships win! I've scribbled down what I've learned from couples in my courtroom. This way you can steer clear of all those alluring R & B songs (hello, Adele!) throwing off your game and sending your heart all over the place on your playlist. (I know, being married to an award-winning love song hit maker. Now you *know* how much love is thought about in our household.) Pop on some Mary J. Blige and stay focused on real love; let's get into what that is (and isn't). Leave the fake stuff for the birds.

Love is not conditional based on
whether things go your way.

For all of you who don't know, the Merriam-Webster dictionary defines *nag* as "constantly harassing someone to do something." Personally, I'm less of a nag and more of a "do it my dang self" kind of gal, but I see nags all up and down my courtroom every day and certainly not exclusively among women.

Stan and Joanne came into my courtroom at their breaking point. Joanne worked in marketing and had a quiet, very likeable personality. She wore little makeup and sported a short fro. Stan had a more high-energy personality. He was very well put together and ex-military. He was used to a very regimented life with lots of rules and high expectations for precision—which had worked out totally fine for his own routine. Stan said Joanne needed more discipline and showed me a schedule he had laid out for her day. She would wake up at six a.m., work out, eat a healthy breakfast, make beds,

and leave for work by 7:07 a.m. He had it timed down to the minute! Joanne never seemed to meet his demands, and he wasn't happy
about it. Joanne wasn't happy either. He had even tried to tell her
how to wear her hair to court that day, she said. I asked Stan about
that, but he couldn't seem to understand why she had a problem
with it. Though you and I understand immediately how bananas
it would be for our man to put us on a diet and do our hair (!!!),
Stan looked genuinely confused. From his standpoint he was helping her. He wanted his loved one to build habits that would support
her physically and mentally. I told him, "Sir, there is another army
cadet out there just waiting for someone like you to love her!" Was
he running the barracks or their home?

Even if he was treating her like a caged bird, he thought it was an
act of love. Stan didn't say this, but that's basically what I got from it.
(Though the more he spoke about it, the louder the huffs and puffs
from the women in the room. Stan should be thankful for our security.) That's all well, Stan, but I had to point out to him that it came
without Joanne consenting to those lifestyle changes. Therefore,
he's not *helping* her, he's *forcing* her. I told him that I understood
why she'd grown resentful and become unhappy in the relationship.
Their love seemed to be a one-way street. (Stan was shocked. I'm not
sure how much he liked me after that.)

Remember these truths about real love and partnership.

Love is a two-way street.

It's clear that Joanne was not the one for Stan. He may have loved
her when they met, but that love wasn't big enough to trump what
he needed in a life partner. Stan probably needed a woman who valued self-discipline as much as he did, perhaps a woman who shared

his military background or was familiar with it from her childhood upbringing or work. He needed a wifely cadet who didn't mind making the bed and cooking for him on his specific timeline.

Many people who love their partner want to uphold the relationship even though there are many differences, so they try to make him or her conform to their needs, preferences, and expectations in order to keep them. Most people don't want to be controlling. It's just hard for them to accept who their partners are. Accept who they are! There will always be areas to improve, but love is understanding that there are differences between you, but you're still going to ride it out side by side and together.

Supporting someone's evolution is different from molding them. As women, we hate more than anything to be treated like we are our man's mother. And we hate even more when they say we are acting like their mother. But sometimes we do try to kick the relationship off by trying to parent him. It can start off as innocent as *Oh, honey, I'll fix your résumé*, and the next thing you're telling him what job to get and what his salary should be. No, no, no—you want to help but not mold. Radically accept a person for who they are from the beginning. We all have room to grow and improve, but don't count on that happening in order for your relationship to work. Your love cannot be conditional on them changing.

Love brings the truth.

Denise, who was an atheist, was dating a Christian man named Joseph. I know it sounds like a disaster . . . and it was. They couldn't have had less in common but, if you can believe this, he didn't know it; yet everyone in my courtroom could see it from a mile away. He was a family man and she didn't want children. His faith was incredibly important to him and she didn't share his beliefs at all yet. It wasn't all Joseph's fault that his love was blind, because she went along with it. She actually went a step further than going with the flow: she'd hid her true feelings from her partner. He soon discovered the truth, and that's how they ended up in my courtroom.

She said that she was afraid of him leaving her if he knew. *Uh, yeah, but that's his right*, I wanted to say. It was akin to betrayal when Joseph discovered her views on religion, because he (rightfully) felt like she had had every opportunity to tell him who she really was. She robbed them both of the opportunity to make decisions for themselves, and let him choose whether love was enough to compromise. He deserved to have exactly what he was looking for without being tricked into a relationship.

This was a classic example of bait and switch. It's okay to change your mind about religious and philosophical beliefs, for example. But don't lie about them because you think someone may not like the real you!

Love evolves.

Over time you will change. So will your man. And that's okay. This is where great communication comes into play. If you're in a long-term relationship, you have to love the newest version of your man and vice versa.

Rosa and Mark married at nineteen years old, and they wound up in *Divorce Court* seven years and three children later. Rosa was a human resources officer and her husband worked in marketing. They met in high school and had been together ever since. Rosa now stood before me at her wit's end and ready to end the marriage. As Rosa spoke, I looked over at Mark and saw him smiling. He had a jovial, friendly personality even in the midst of the seriousness of their presence in court. I said to him, "I've never seen anyone quite so happy to be in divorce court, sir." He was admittedly likeable. I'm sure that's what had attracted Rosa to him from the beginning. Rosa went on to explain that Mark was a constant prankster in their marriage. He would spray fart spray around her while she was sleeping. He would hide her car keys before it was time to go to work. Basically, Rosa didn't have three kids; she had four! Rosa was tired of games, and Mark was not listening to her wishes. Mark, on the other hand, thought he was hilarious. He thought all of the things he was doing were harmless and that she should lighten up. He told me, "She used to think I was funny."

Here's what Mark needed to understand, Rosa was now twenty-six years old and what she thought was funny at nineteen she didn't find funny now. I told Mark, "It's okay to have fun and be funny, but find something that she thinks is funny—not just you!"

This is where learning to hear your love's love language and keeping current with how they like to be loved is key. Understand that how a person desires to be loved may change over time. Nothing stays stagnant; recognize that and evolve too.

People Lie, Patterns Don't

The hard part about love is that when it feels good, even when we know it's wrong, we don't want to be right. Luther Ingram's song has stood the test of time for a reason. I can't tell you the number of strong, successful women who have asked me questions about love that they would have known the answers to if they weren't blindly chasing after a man who didn't want or deserve to be chased.

Disciplined decision-making is the strongest form of self-love. At times that will mean walking away from men who give you goose bumps. It can also mean refusing to ignore the signs that your handsome and accomplished bae isn't emotionally ready.

In criminal law, people who harm others are notorious for returning to the scene of the crime, even though every crime show indicates that that's a horrible idea and will lead to their capture. Even still, they do it all the time. Perhaps the rush of adrenaline is too good to ignore. Or maybe those who choose to return have convinced themselves that they aren't like the others. No matter the reasoning, they almost always get caught.

The same is true for romantic relationships. Women who know a man is no good or uninterested in the level of commitment she's looking for continue to open their minds, hearts, and bodies. And when that man proves himself to be exactly who his actions said he was, that same woman will go crying to her girlfriends about how he had the audacity to hurt her. At a certain point, there has to be a level of accountability we have with ourselves and with each other.

Love should not shield us from accountability by clouding our judgment and keeping us from seeing things we would see in any other aspect of our lives. It's called *confirmation bias*. We see what we want to see because reality is harder than living a lie. If you are someone who chronically misses red flags, you need an external tool: detecting patterns. When the FBI is building a profile on someone, one of the first things they do is track and analyze someone's patterns. What do you consistently do, think, avoid, etc.?

Assessing trends in behavior can tell us things about someone that they haven't fully admitted to themselves. Patterns don't lie. Patterns tell us what smooth words and perfectly curated dates never can. Read between the lines to see what the patterns are revealing. A man who is consistently late to your dates is someone who doesn't prioritize you. A man who regularly berates service staff lacks human decency and has a violent ego. And on the flip side, a man who remembers little details and meaningfully incorporates them into dates isn't "too nice," he cares about you. A man who is courteous to others isn't a "punk"—he knows when not to pick a fight and how to conduct himself in your presence.

If you have a pattern of dating men whom you know can't meet your needs and allowing yourself to get your hopes up that things will change, this is something to be addressed. Stop blaming the clown for being a clown. Instead, ask yourself why you keep going back to the circus and find a new hobby.

Your World Still Rotates Without Him

Many women go into the dating arena wanting to find "their everything." *When I find my man, he's going to be my everything!* Yeah, we're cancelling that attitude right here . . . Destiny's Child was on to something when they said, " 'Cause I depend on me." It's important that you have a life outside of your relationship, and men love it too. The key to your happiness should never be in the hands of another person. Hello, Ms. Independent, don't forget about all the other good stuff you have going on in your life just because a man enters the equation.

Have you ever had a friend who as soon as she got a new man— I mean they are only a few months in—she starts dropping plans, suddenly her hobbies cease to exist, and she can't meet you for golf anymore, nor can she hold a complete conversation with you when you are hanging out because she has to be readily available if and when he calls? Girl, no. You can be a doting partner while still having a full life of your own outside of your man. I guarantee you that he wants these things for you too.

When you both have your own worlds going on, there's also less conflict. Many couples would get along better if they just had more space. Let men know that you're a busy woman. This 1) communicates that he should be planning dates earlier in advance and 2) reminds him that you value yourself and your time, because, trust me, he values his. Whether it's a night out with his boys or a company event, he doesn't want to put his life on pause for someone, and neither should you. Your paths can still be parallel without being identical.

I get it if your life is pretty much set. You paid for "the rocks that you got, the clothes you're wearing, and the house you live in," right, and all you need now is a man. You're feeling, *Hey, Faith, I'm just trying to chill out.* Well then, you shouldn't complain when all you're getting attention from is Booker at the barber shop who throws white parties even in the dead of winter. And if you're just sitting around doing the same routine year in and year out without growing and just worrying about a man, that's not going to work. In general, it's a good idea to get yourself involved in new things to keep evolving.

As I've said about your dating life, I'll say again about your relationship life: do things that interest you outside of the love space. It's just healthy. And I'm not talking about just tending to your responsibilities with work and family. As children, we're taught to try new things and how important balance is, and then it all goes out the window when we're adults. There's no adult to enroll us on the track team. It's now up to you to create the life you want. Be vibrant, do things that you're not so good at, rediscover old talents, and commit to constant growth. The young you was good at karate or loved crafting—get involved again. Or how about now trying aerial yoga? Just do something. You'll have an exciting life with or without a man, and any man will then know that he better come correct!

Part III

---◈---

WHEN CONFLICT
COMES KNOCKING

Chapter 10

Iyanla, Fix Our Life!

"Peace is not the absence of conflict but the presence of creative alternatives for responding to conflict."

—DOROTHY THOMPSON

A relationship is like the law of gravity: what goes up must come down. That's the law of love. A healthy relationship is full of constant synergy, but don't get it twisted. As we've discussed, no relationship is without conflict, but how you handle conflict is the best test of a relationship's longevity. This is the stuff that makes for nineties R & B music (which I so happen to love!) so I'll let New Edition make it plain:

Sunny days, everybody loves them
Tell me, baby, can you stand the rain?

The timing of the honeymoon-phase-wear-off varies for each relationship, so social media baes beware! When things are digital, everything is airbrushed. It's not until time passes and you start letting your guard down that you become more aware of your significant other's habits and patterns—*and likewise*! Suddenly, who you thought you couldn't go a day without is working on your last nerves. Or your partner is picking at the smallest things with you. In many relationships you'll find that you're paired with someone completely different from you on many levels. Stop trying to avoid this. It's inevitable and understandable given that you grew up in different environments, with different upbringings, and have different experiences and varying perspectives on life. The best job experiences I've had were not the ones where I was the smartest in the room or where everyone agreed with me. What made the work interesting, the conversations stimulating, and the casework engaging was working with people who had different points of view offering their opinion.

If you're looking for someone just like you and who will do everything the way you want things done, then save yourself the trouble of pursuing marriage and start making your dinner reservations for one. Marriage isn't for everyone, and it certainly isn't for someone who needs their views constantly adhered to. Winning in love isn't about having the last word or proving a point months after an argument. It's about identifying what will make the relationship stronger and walking boldly toward that.

What Are We Even Fighting About?

Initial conflicts can feel a lot like landing a plane. You might go in thinking it's technical, easy peasy: someone was hurt, the other person apologizes, apology accepted, and *boom*: landed! In reality so many things can get in the way and cloud vision and judgment for both of you. Sometimes your significant other doesn't apologize immediately. They don't agree that they did something wrong. *Or* both parties feel hurt and no one wants to go first. Or, even worse, you're hurt and decide to be passive-aggressive about it, so the best way for your partner to solve the problem is to play a game of Clue (!) and figure out what's wrong.

Small irritants left unaddressed become big problems, and pet peeves grow into major disputes. True colors begin to show, and it gets harder and harder to fake the funk. Your once calm, cool, and collected boyfriend now has road rage. Or maybe he was Mr. *GQ* on your first dates, and now he's always in basketball shorts and tank tops. And vice versa! Before you may have tidied up extra, but now you're lax, with dirty laundry thrown every which way around your apartment. Your secret, single behavior is now on full display! There's a difference between small quirks and major mismatches in values. Figuring this out early is key!

Note to My Sistas

In the case of Black women and women of color generally, conflict can be a hard space to navigate. Disrespect toward us has been so normalized—especially when we consider the trope of "angry Black women," a status many of us want to avoid like a kid avoids the dentist—that we are more susceptible to accepting mistreatment. It's important not to accept what doesn't serve you and to trust that your soulmate isn't someone hell-bent on tearing you down. Trust that there's a plan for your life that includes you being loved and taken care of, and I don't mean solely financially.

When the airbrushed and curated behavior wears off, you'll see your real person show up. When you do, you're left with three options: you can accept, reject, or rebuild your man.

Accept Him

Let's look at Yessica and Frank. Yessica was a vegan and adamantly opposed to eating any meat or dairy products. When she met Frank, she knew he was not vegan but she decided it wasn't a deal breaker for her. They eventually moved in together, and *she* decided that for Frank's own good he should also stop eating meat or dairy. They started having arguments over him sneaking and eating cheese! Yessica explained to me that dairy was one of the worst things you could put in your body and that she was trying to help Frank see the light. I told her that was Frank's choice to make. By forcing him to become vegan she was essentially parenting him, and he would eventually resent her for it and find someone who would accept him for who he was: a cheese head! I told Frank to go home and order a pizza! If Yessica gave him a hard time about it, then she wasn't ready, willing, and able to accept him for who he was.

Ladies, what's important are his core values. If he has your core values, then accept him for who he is. There are going to be some differences. If he's a night person and you're a morning person, that's okay. If you're a vegan and you've decided you're okay with dating a steak lover, don't turn your nose up at the sight of his filet mignon. It's our differences that make us special and unique—we're not all supposed to be the same.

Reject Him

But if the misalignment is in a critical area, move on. Everyone isn't for everyone. If he wants to live in rural Kentucky on a farm and your family and line of work is based in Los Angeles or New York, reject him clearly and kindly so that you can both move on in ease. If he tells you he never wants kids, and you know you want children, then you know you aren't compatible. These are red flags for you to get out early, not for you to "rise to the challenge" and see if you can change his mind.

Rebuild Him

This is the worst of the three. And, unfortunately, it's all too common. This is the "I like you. Now change." category. Nothing will push a person farther away than a woman coming in to rebuild a man into who she thinks he needs to be.

I have had countless cases where women come in and have a laundry list of things they don't like about their significant others but then say in exasperation, "And, on top of it all, he still won't propose!" Sis, what? If things are so bad, why do you want a ring?

Don't assume that if he proposes all will be well! After he's been subjected to crying, arguing, persuasion, and cajoling all in an effort to be someone you want him to be, he'll feel parented, and you'll feel ignored, like you're not being heard.

Here's what doesn't work: nagging, complaining, or manipulating. People can change and make improvements, but they rarely will when a gun is put to their head. Think about it: when someone is under duress they are going to say what they need to say to get out of the pressure zone. You demand that he go to the early morning service every Sunday because you sing in the choir, but in reality he's secretly playing video games on his phone! He loves God all right, but he'd rather worship him at the night service.

When the pressure's off, they revert back to who they really are anyway. Don't stay to try to change him; and this includes all who think you're not "putting up with it," but yet here you are still complaining to him. That's a recipe for disappointment on your side and leads to resentment from him.

It won't take long for you to realize whether your man is willing to meet you halfway. The second it becomes clear your non-negotiables can't be met, it's time for you to create space for the relationship you need. That means no sticking around for a year or longer hoping he'll change his mind or get it together. You're only prolonging the inevitable. True freedom comes from seeing people as they are—not as you want them to be.

Checking in with and revising your non-negotiables (as we discussed in chapter 4) over time as the relationship develops honors your evolution and keeps you on track to ensure you're with someone who nourishes and complements you. Otherwise, you can be in for some rude awakenings…

Whip out that paper and pen or your phone again and review that list of what you can't live without (also from chapter 4!). Do it now. Do it ASAP. Keep this list in a place that is easily accessible to you. You'll save yourself a lot of fights and agony if this list is kept close by as a reminder. These are the sections I've used:

Updated Non-Negotiables—(such as spiritually minded, independent, traveler, financial stability, non-smoker, character—honest and forthcoming)

Updated "Bonuses" and Things I've Always Wanted but Can Compromise On—(like living in a specific city, pets, holiday traditions, six-pack abs)

Things I Don't *Want Long Term* (long-distance relationship, lack of boundaries around extended family, character issues—lying and dishonesty)

When you begin to envision sharing a life with someone, don't get so lost in the ruse of potential that you become Barbara the Builder. And don't try to change someone who doesn't have an interest in changing. It sets him up for resentment, and you up for failure.

Now that you've gotten past that, let's get back to how to handle the inevitable: conflict.

Conflict and disagreements will happen in every relationship. We're all unique individuals and are not likely to always agree with everything or with anyone—not with family, friends, coworkers, or especially with love interests. Just because you do something differently doesn't make it wrong.

How you handle yourself and also how you handle the heart of the person you are supposed to love during conflict will tell you a lot. It's easy to be good to your person when you're on vacation or when you're out for a night on the town, but how you treat each other when you're going through a difficult time is what matters most.

As Bishop T. D. Jakes explained in one of his recent sermons, when a pilot finds herself landing a plane, she can sometimes hit turbulent conditions. This is where you either buckle in and trust the co-pilot (the other person in the relationship) or you realize that you aren't on the same page and choose to jump out to save yourself. In other words, when you go through tumultuous times in your relationship, it takes communication and effort to survive.

A lot of times when conflict arises, people go into self-preservation mode and couples become each other's adversaries. When you're in a relationship, you're still in partnership, even when there are disagreements. You never become the other's enemy. Your job is to figure out what the conflict means and what the solution is. Sometimes the conflict just means you are coming from a different perspective. The desire to "win" the conflict should not be the focus when you're on the same team. The goal of resolving conflict is to come out with a better understanding of who each other is, better insight into yourself, improved teamwork as a couple, all while exposing unaddressed personal issues.

You may not be able to control what happened, but you can always control your reaction. Often I see the worst conflicts are rarely about the initial action that made someone upset. No, it's more often about how disrespectful you two got. It's about not fighting fair.

Communication can break down at a moment's notice. All it takes is one crossed signal or unexpressed assumption for the spiral of attack and defense to begin and the lines of transmission to break down.

High emotions do not justify bad behavior. How couples deal with conflict in their relationship is the number one indicator of whether it's going to last. You won't always agree, but the important thing is learning to open yourself up to ideas and new ways of doing things and that you are respectful in the ways in which you disagree. This is what opens you up for a relationship that withstands turbulence and forms a strong, lasting bond.

You've heard the saying "A drunk mind speaks sober thoughts," and I'm here to tell you so does an angry one. In a courtroom the term "held in contempt" is used to deter misconduct and ensure the judge can preside in a respectful environment. When someone disobeys or *dishonors* the court of law, they are held in contempt. That gives me the power to basically shut them up, including physically removing them from the courtroom if necessary. In real life, there's no gavel or sanction for rude behavior. Instead of turning to a judge for backup, real life requires setting and sticking to your boundaries.

It's shocking what two people who once loved each other can say and do in fits of rage. News flash: someone who really loves you doesn't work to push your buttons. Most couples I see in *Divorce Court* are there because they don't have a clue about understanding each other in times of conflict or communicating effectively about their different perspectives. They did the worst thing you can do in the heat of conflict: said and did things to intentionally hurt the other.

Kameron and Andrea appeared before me after two years in a serious relationship, but there was only one problem: Kameron was still legally married! He and his estranged wife had been separated for three years, but he claimed she refused to sign the papers. (I told him he was in *Divorce Court* with the wrong person!) Andrea said she was understanding about his divorce delays (for two years, sis?), and so she decided to remain in a committed relationship with him. They were standing before me because they didn't know how to manage conflict in their relationship, and the hurtful rhetoric had driven them to a point of no return. In their latest argument, when Kameron got upset with Andrea, he told her she was nothing but his mistress anyway! Ouch.

Andrea, in an act of revenge, talked about the small size of Kameron's manhood to one of his neighbors. Yep, she went all the way there! Talk about below the belt. The desire to say the most hurtful thing or one-up the other in the midst of conflict is a relationship assassin. Going tit-for-tat is a slippery slope. Pettiness and revenge are two sides of the same dangerous coin, and that type of currency isn't accepted in the kinds of high-value relationships we're trying to call forth.

Hurt people will always hurt people in an effort to find comfort in their misery. What Kameron and Andrea didn't realize was that the short-term satisfaction they received in going for the jugular was keeping the vicious cycle going. There are some things that should never be said. Some deeds that should never be done. Because when the smoke clears after a nine-alarm fire, the damage has already been done. You can't un-ring those bells. Instead of fighting to the death—killing and draining the relationship—over who is the bigger, better person, how about making an agreement that you either rise higher or separate from each other's toxicity.

Pro Tip: Neither of You Are Psychic

There are a lot of people who can't handle the choppy waters so they jump ship immediately. Some people keep changing partners to avoid changing themselves.

If you take only one thing away from this book, understand that knowing how to communicate is your *best* friend. It's the secret sauce to navigating and *preserving* your relationships (not just your love relationships). We live in a three-dimensional world, so there will be times where we have missing or inaccurate information that, when unchecked, can cause us to spin out of control. Clarity is the antidote and will help you make thoughtful and mature decisions no matter what you're faced with in challenging times with your sweetie.

Before I ever set foot in the courtroom, I stop and assess what information I have to support my position. You can do the same in matters of your heart. As a judge and attorney, information keeps me levelheaded and focused less on my emotion. Formulating my thoughts without assumptions muddying things up allows me better judgment. When in a time of conflict with your bae, ask yourself four key questions before talking to them.

The Four-Question Rule

Let me share something with you: I've talked to hundreds of men about their relationship needs. The one common theme they express wanting in their love lives? Peace. They do not like arguments. In most cases, the last thing they want in their relationship is to rock the boat. So often these disagreements come down to miscommunication and lack of clarity—not intentional malice. You have to be comfortable enough to openly share what you want and don't want and allow people room to grow and learn from mistakes. When you and your partner come together to share a life, you'll soon realize that there are differing perspectives on what constitutes something offensive.

We all learn about love through different life examples; what is unacceptable to one may have been normalized in their childhood or in previous relationships for the other. This doesn't make it okay, and I'm never a proponent for settling (hence the name of this book!) or sacrificing important standards and boundaries. A mismatch in expectations may mean your values aren't aligned. Spend time reflecting on whether this is a learning moment or a habit, and have patience with the journey.

We often expect our significant others to be mind-readers instead of honestly evaluating how they may be feeling or perceiving things. Perhaps the relationship can still be salvaged if you spend time hearing each other instead of talking *at* each other. Here's how to self-evaluate:

1. **Have I communicated my expectations in a clear way that he understood?** Oftentimes communication breaks down because of something as simple as an unclear message. Little things turn into big things when we assume a miscommunication is intentionally malicious or when we feel unfairly chastised. Your man deserves the same grace that you want when you fall short—especially if there's a chance he never truly knew to begin with. Next time before jumping into accusations or assumptions, sincerely ask what his perception

of things is and check for where something may have been missed.

2. **Am I projecting unsaid expectations on my partner?** We all enter relationships with assumptions about how they're supposed to work and how we feel our partner is supposed to speak, dress, drive, eat, do laundry, set the table, etc. All of this is what we perceive as correct. For most of us, it's not that we expect our partner to be perfect, but rather that we would like them to do things exactly as we would expect them to. Frustration abounds as two people unconsciously try to make the other person conform to what each perceives as the "right" way to be. Assumptions rob you of the communication process. If you assume you know, you won't ask. Almost always these assumptions, conjectures, and expectations are the source of misunderstandings.

3. **Am I reacting or responding?** When you react, you let others control you. When you respond, you put yourself in control. When you sense yourself reacting, take a deep breath and try not to take any action until you can sense and relax your body. If you do react—or even overreact—it's an opportunity to learn about yourself, what's triggering the reaction, so you can control it the next time. Overreacting comes from emotional patterns we've developed over time. That's why we get swept away in the moment—these are automatic reactions that happen to keep us out of harm's way when we don't have time to think about what's going on. So next time this reaction happens to you, watch as soon as the emotion begins to take over. Without judging yourself, take a deep breath and ask yourself, where is this coming from? The answer will come to you. When it does, it could be that this fear is linked to a subconscious belief you may not be aware of, a belief that

may not be valid. This gives you an opportunity to look at that belief again to examine it. Remember, people and situations are powerless without your reaction.

4. **What does a resolution look like for me?** The end goal is to come to an understanding that makes sense for your relationship moving forward. Sometimes the resolution is compromise, and sometimes it's you being willing to try something new and be open-minded. How you communicate during these times is still key. People will close off if they feel they're under attack, and when that happens you can't deal with the issue at hand. You're dealing more with the emotion of how you're feeling in that moment. When communicating in a respectful and loving way, it's easier to navigate these waters together. The best way to deal with an issue in your relationship is to share your feelings about it at the appropriate time without holding grudges. Taking time to collect your thoughts is one thing, but delaying conflict, remaining silent while secretly seething, just leads to bigger conflict later.

By taking the time to walk through these questions *before* going toe to toe, you are approaching your relationship like a woman with an investment. You wouldn't fall asleep at the wheel or stunt the growth of a financial opportunity because of the potential rewards on the other side. Treat your romantic relationship the same way. Nurture and foster it. Be smart and prepared so that you can attract a partner willing to do the same.

Tone, Timing, and Temperament

In a relationship you and your partner are teammates, and the tone in which you speak to each other affects your performance. Winning should look a lot less like proving your point and more like creating space for changed behavior and greater understanding. Imagine watching a football game where the quarterback and wide receiver of the same team begin beefing on the field. It would be chaos, because it derails them from driving the overarching mission forward. When they do have conflict, they want to resolve it in a way that betters the team and moves them in the right direction. Similarly, to stay on the same page we have to make time in the locker room for addressing any concerns in order to move forward in a healthy way. As Jay-Z said, "No one wins when the family feuds."

When the endgame is growth, you operate differently. This will bring out a next level in maturity in your relationship, and it will bear fruit. When you come into a disagreement or dispute with facts, it's more likely to end with solutions than shouting. And this approach will serve you in platonic, familial, and working relationships as well. Tone is something that consistently comes through in my courtrooms, because people don't know how to speak to their loved ones when angry without blowing up. Learn from that, ladies. If you can't speak to someone you "love" without it coming off like a street fight between strangers, then rethink your definition of love. How you say what you say matters. As my mama would say, "Check your tone!"

If you've seen the film *Bad Boys*, you watched Martin Lawrence's character "woosah" his way out of stressful situations. It was advice from his therapist on how to ground and still himself; how to ensure the right *timing* of when and how he responded to frustrating situations. We laugh or minimize its power, but taking a beat to be still and calm down is so critical for both parties. In addition to making sure you have a chance to breathe, also ensure your partner has that same opportunity. Just because you've been plotting and planning for this conversation doesn't mean you get to catch them off guard and jump into presentation mode. Whether fresh out of work or in the heat of their anger, it can be jarring not to have a say in how a disagreement discussion transpires. In law, at least we subpoena people and allow them notice to build their own case. There's nothing wrong with returning to a conversation when initial anger has subsided because, again, the goals are clarity and solutions.

You may also want to state to your partner how you like to be communicated with when there's a problem—everyone's process should be respected, including yours, and the more information you can provide him, the better.

Temperament is another major component of how to establish peace. Your mouth can be saying one thing, but if your arms are folded, you are rolling your eyes, or your overall presence is abysmal, then your partner will begin to feel a way about how present and open you are to hearing them. This isn't a monologue, so we have to keep the lines of communication open. Let's set the tone for how we engage.

Okay, now that you've got an idea of how to handle the tone, time, and temperament, and you've also asked yourself the Four Questions and are clear on possible solutions, here are some dos and don'ts to keep in mind when you jump into the convo with your man.

Dos:

- Take the time to breathe deeply before starting the conversation. This will help clear your mind so emotion doesn't cloud your judgment.

- Use body language and words that affirm you're having this conversation because you care. Speak the truth in love.
- Be willing to pause the conversation if things get heated to collect your thoughts.
- When you ask him a question, be an active listener—listen to understand, not to respond. Don't interject with petty ad-libs every time you hear something you don't like. For a conversation to be productive it doesn't have to happen all at once. You can introduce the topic at hand and present your facts, but if the argument is going in circles, pausing is your friend! It allows what's been said to marinate, and you both can come back even more levelheaded and possibly empathetic to your partner's needs and desires. Sometimes I even suggest assigning some "homework" so that if you take some space from each other, you're using that time away wisely. For example, journaling about where the conversation is going or even speaking one-on-one with a therapist or other third-party source can be great tools for understanding.

<u>Don'ts:</u>

- Don't discuss serious relationship issues when either one of you is not in a space to do so (tired, hungry, or rushing). Discern whether it's the right time.
- Don't interrupt your partner when they are speaking, and establish that everyone's speaking time is respected.
- Don't make accusations; instead, ask open-ended questions and respond accordingly (How do you understand the situation? What's a good solution look like for you?).

It's perfectly acceptable to say things like: *Can we talk about this later after I've had time to gather my thoughts?* Or *I don't have the energy to respond to this right now. I can do so later when I've had time to recharge.* Or even *I need some space so I can think clearly about the best way to respond.*

Being smart in relationships requires doing something different. You've heard the expression "Insanity is doing the same thing over and over again and expecting different results." Don't bring the same childish behaviors to relationships where you desire a different outcome. Even when you've been wrong, your tone, timing, and temperament are everything! How you say what you say, when you say it, and the environment you say it in will all affect how your man receives that message. If your goal is reconciliation, then you can't explode every time you get shaken up. Have complete control of your inside so that no one can manipulate you out of your character.

A couple of months ago I was at lunch with my girlfriend, and she was rehashing an argument she had had with her boyfriend of five months. He had gone out to drinks with an ex without telling her, and she felt betrayed. I resonated with her feelings, because who hasn't been *there* before. It was clear this was making her second-guess what else he might be keeping from her. "He lied by omission and now we aren't speaking! How can I trust him?" While I empathized with those initial feelings, I told her that I couldn't understand how it had been so blown up to where they were giving each other the silent treatment months later. That's not a resolution.

Here's what happened:

Her boyfriend had arrived at her home around ten p.m. and didn't bring up where he had been. My friend also didn't ask. But while he was in the shower she searched his phone and text messages—**mistake number one**! She ultimately found exactly what she was looking for: a text from his ex that said, "Great to see you. Glad you're happy." When her boyfriend came out of the bathroom, she went off on him about trust and honesty—**mistake number two!** He decided to leave, and they hadn't spoken since then. I decided to walk my girl through some questions.

> Me: "If you wanted to know where he'd been, why didn't you ask?"
>
> Her: "He should have known I wanted to know."

Okay, so he's psychic.

> Me: "Could it be that he grabbed innocent drinks with his ex for something completely unrelated to their relationship? And what if, during that conversation, he told her about you as part of his happiness? Sure, he didn't tell you in advance, but could it be he was going to tell you but didn't get a chance to because you turned into *CSI*??"

I thought I could squeeze a chuckle out of her, but the girl wasn't having that.

> Her: "He should have known to just be straightforward so that we are on the same page and I don't have to find out elsewhere what he's been up to."
>
> Me: "You mean like in his personal cell phone?"

She didn't have a solid response because she had been playing the game the way it had been taught to her. In a world of reality television and WorldstarHipHop, responding out of anger has been so normalized. But it's not normal for everyone, and many people will straight up walk away.

Next, we went over dos and don'ts in talking through disagreements, to retrace her steps and see where things could have gone differently so that she'd end up with real information. As we discussed, the issue took on another form when she started going through her man's phone. But that was her fact-finding mission, so we examined her actions right after she saw the text. The first thing she could have done was to back away from the phone and *breathe*. This way when he came out of the shower, they could have had a real conversation. Instead of jumping to accusations and launching into a one-woman show where he couldn't get a word in, she should have started with an open-ended question like "I know you went for drinks with your ex. Why didn't you tell me?"

She could have let *him* tell *her* where his logic came from so that she could respond to the merit of his feelings as opposed to the story of deceit and betrayal that she came up with. When you become the listener rather than the accuser, that opens up the opportunity for you to let him know you don't need him to protect you with white lies because you value transparency over anything. In the courtroom, we call proceedings "hearings" because the emphasis is on listening before we take the subsequent action. If you're the only one speaking, that's not a dialogue. No grown adult wants to be chastised in a one-way discussion.

My girl was still on the fence about all of this. In her eyes, he had done wrong, so it was on him to be the bigger person instead of walking away from the conversation altogether. And I didn't blame her! The best move for him was to tell her in advance so there would be no tea leaves to read from. My girl had turned into Usain Bolt— so quick to run and jump to conclusions. Listen, she couldn't control what he did; only how she reacted to him. And the way she responded didn't create space for communication or reconciliation—if that was in fact what she wanted. If he had stayed that night, she would have continued to yell at him, and out of anger he might have said or done things to make the situation worse. "Wouldn't you rather he step away to gather himself?" I asked her. "Could it possibly have been a sign of respect for you and not an attack on you?" She hadn't thought of it like that, and now she was rethinking the in-your-face antics she had thrown at him. There she was with a good man who cherished her and possibly hadn't done anything wrong, but she hadn't given him the *benefit of the doubt*.

If you're ever in this type of situation after reading this book, you'll be fine. You will follow the Four-Question Rule; then you will get the clarity in yourself and from him that's needed to move forward. You won't jump to conclusions every time your man shows up late or doesn't call or when something appears off. You'll know communication is the way. That communication will end with some direction on how either or both of you can adjust your behavior and avoid similar conflict in the future.

When you land on solutions, focus on that! There's a saying, "What happens here, stays here. What's learned here, leaves here." No need to keep rehashing what he said or you said. It won't heal the relationship to keep holding tight and revisiting the anger you felt or baby the issue like it's a child that needs care. We know this, but still, in the moment of frustration we must enforce this on ourselves. Let a moment be a moment, not a monument. Let go of the minutia and walk toward the evolved version of yourself.

I've known women in their thirties and forties who were smart, successful, and yet obsessive over the smallest things, like missed texts. By losing their cool, they handed over the power to a man and erased decades of hard-won confidence. What happened to their cool? Where'd it go? I've had to help many a Bernie learn to exhale...but we want to do it before the car is set on fire.

Remember that we all grow and bloom in loving, nurturing relationships. Remember that you're both imperfect people and will have good and bad days. Commit to the relationship and do your part on your side of the equation to bring your best self, and allow them room to do their part on theirs. Little faults deserve little reactions. Big faults deserve big ones. What is never helpful is when one person feels that they're trying hard to learn about their partner, and the other person is impatient and naggy. Ugh, we've all been there. Empathy will take our relationships further than impatience ever could. We've all had a supervisor who couldn't stop micromanaging; someone who is always looking over your shoulder and never lets you live down a misstep, even when you're really trying. As a grown adult, it feels insulting to not be trusted. That's in a working relationship, so imagine how it feels coming from a lover whom you see as an equal.

Use the tools of communication to get what you want from your relationship, even if it means agreeing to disagree respectfully. I don't advise the "forgive and forget" trope because that can lead to pent-up frustration. However, if you leave the conversation agreeing to work things out, then commit to that—not parenting. That means not bringing up old arguments unprovoked. Do not resort to sarcasm. Do not use open-ended questions to do your dirty work. If the argument is brought back up, it's in an affirming way—"We promised each other after that last argument to commit to this. Are we upholding that?"—as opposed to "See, this is why I should never have taken you back!"

Your partner may fall short in delivering on the agreed-upon solutions, but you'll be able to tell whether it's for lack of effort/interest or simply the need for more time. When your iPhone updates its software, it asks to be plugged into a power source so that it can completely reset. People aren't machines. We need just as much support in unlearning and relearning one another's needs.

Crazy in Love

Reclaiming our sanity after big conflicts and moments of passion can be one of the hardest parts of a relationship. In the face of gaslighting and outright mean behavior, love can make us feel crazy.

When you do master the art of hearing your partner and, in turn, being heard by them, you unlock a new level of maturity. This is the grown and sexy that leads to fulfilled and long-lasting marriages. I hear so many people eager to make the promise of marriage, but they haven't put in the work to prepare for all that goes with it. Everyone says that marriage is hard work, but few want to do The Work. Never forget that it's what you do on the rainy days that sets the foundation for how happy and satisfied you will be in a relationship. As I've mentioned, don't pray that it's easy—because it's in the challenging times that we can learn and grow the most as a unit; pray for the will and commitment to constantly show up and grow together.

It will feel amazing to be in a relationship where you trust your significant other enough to be your full self. Knowing that when you are honest about your desires and boundaries, your partner will welcome that with open arms because they love you enough to nurture your needs...*Phew!* It's life-changing, girl, especially if you've been used to men who make excuses, ghost you, or refuse to take accountability. Love yourself enough to get smart in your relationships so that you can draw in someone who wants the same. When you find someone who is willing to sit in the trenches with you, don't let go and *bloom*!

Chapter 11

I Can Do Bad All by Myself

*"You've got to learn to leave the table
when love's no longer being served."*

—NINA SIMONE

Not all conflict can be talked through. Sometimes you keep having the same arguments about things so important, you can't get past them. Sometimes you find yourself months—or even years—into a relationship with a man before you realize that he is a complete mismatch with your non-negotiables. Especially when you factor in societal pressures, many of us women will try to push past the pain with the belief that this is what makes relationships challenging and that every couple faces this tension. I'm here to tell you it's not true.

Sure, every relationship comes with its own work, but that shouldn't involve quelling things that are important to you. The point of writing down your non-negotiables is so that you are crystal clear on what is worth compromising on and what can't be fixed. Some people are great, just not great for you; the same way every puzzle piece is important but it won't fit just anywhere. Know what you're looking for and what you're not, so that you can walk away from anything not serving you.

A big part of suffering and angst in dating stems from trying to figure out the ambiguity. There's so much stringing along that happens when both people in the relationship aren't eyes wide open to what's happening. Men lie, women lie, actions don't! If his actions and words are contradicting, then his actions are the only thing that matters. It doesn't matter what he "promised" or "what you see in him." Someone telling you they love you when their actions say otherwise is not enough. As Toni Braxton sang, "Love shoulda brought you home last night." Don't be the only one fighting in the ring.

I'm not saying it's easy to let go of a man, especially when there's history, but it's impossible to get to the love you deserve when you're holding onto what's not. You may be spending precious time in your life on him with the hope that you will be able to show him your value and he'll have an epiphany and give you more attention or care. So you're jumping through hoops to plead your case, but he's not matching your energy. You call him the second you get out of work, but he needs space. You're texting paragraphs, and he's leaving you on read. And the only reason you're holding on is because of the good times that you shared in the past.

Trust me, I understand it's easier said than done, sis, but I also have to keep it real. Discipline really does have to be a major force in your relationships. You should never be going above and beyond for someone's bare minimum. If when you're together he says all the right things, but when you're apart it's like you have to remind him you exist, nope he's not the *right* one. You're only his choice when it's convenient. Being wanted is easy. It's being valued that's the key. He may call you once a month for sex—he wants you. He may text you to say hello but never picks up the actual phone to call you. (Texts are a low bar.) Perhaps he wants to keep you as an option. Minimal effort deserves a minimal response from you. When you're valued, you know it. The effort will match it. You should not be expending more energy than he is. Early on this will weed out the ones who are not ready, willing, able, and available for long-term relationships.

Stop trying to read the tea leaves, ladies. It's really not that difficult to discern! You deserve to be with someone who wants all of you and gives you all of himself.

If he's texting and calling every now and then with no consistency or substance (especially if he was doing it more often before), he's not ready, willing, able, and available for you. If someone is slow to initiate communication or only calls you occasionally, it means they are not interested *enough*. Act as if life is rigged in your favor and take it as a good sign that you have clarity now. You can move forward knowing the man who matches your ready, able, and available energy is on the way, and this current guy is not it!

There are plenty of men out there who want love as much as you do. When you give them the space to come to you, that's what happens. The easy way out is hounding someone—we want to take control instead of waiting patiently, which requires deep levels of focus. But if we want to love stronger, then we have to show up differently. We have to be smarter and believe what we see. Don't lose sleep over a man who is clearly giving you his *divided* attention. What it really means is he's not really available. Life goes on.

Dump Him!

Stop calling, block, exit the premises for good, but do whatever you need to do at this moment to quit any unhealthy relationship that you have been entangled in with a person who will never be your partner. *Unhealthy* could mean as bad as a stomach flu or just not the right balance to keep your mind, body, and soul good. I know he may have certain nice features, but if you know that he's not the man for you, then start outlining and implementing the blueprint for your exit strategy now. Staying in a bad relationship takes precious time and energy away from the person who matters most: you. Some relationships aren't bad, but they are bad for you. Meaning they are simply not good enough. And that's okay, because your standards are high now. No more swimming in the shallow end of the pool. You are ready to roll in the deep.

When you walk away from a negative, one-sided, low vibrational relationship—you *win*.

I'll never forget my first serious relationship. Randy and I dated long distance while I was in law school. He would take his weekends off twice a month and fly to see me. So for a long-distance relationship, we actually saw each other a lot. It worked out well initially! The problem was that every time we saw each other, it was like a honeymoon. We never got to spend that time together that would allow us to see each other unfiltered—stressed, rushing, juggling schedules, etc. As I became swamped with schoolwork, his visits became less of a treat and more like a burden in my already busy world. He was a great guy, but I had to focus on studying, while he wanted to go check out the latest restaurant. He had a busy job too, so it became better if he visited a little less, and he agreed. Absence makes the heart grow fonder, right?

Well, one summer I decided to play the nice girlfriend and take a summer job in his city so we could be closer. I immediately sensed something was off when Randy picked me up from the airport. He was incredibly distant and dropped me off at my summer apartment abruptly with no desire or plan to spend more time together. I thought he was just having a bad day, but when this behavior continued, I knew something was off. I saw him four times the entire summer. *Four!*

My summer roommate was a flight attendant named Don who was also from Louisiana; we'd known each other since I was in college. He knew how excited I was to take this summer job and spend more time with Randy in the same city (finally!). I remember that entire summer whenever Don would come back from trips he would see me—on the couch. Whenever he'd go out to dinner with friends on the weekends he'd come back and see me—on the couch. He started inviting me out with his group. I didn't know anyone else in town really besides him. He obviously noticed I was never out with Randy. He never saw him the entire summer, but Don never said a word. He never asked where he was or what happened or how things were going. I was embarrassed, and it made me incredibly grateful to have a friend who just pretended not to notice. When I did tell Don at the end of the summer, he listened intently and said, "Well, it's better to know now rather than later."

The relationship with Randy was obviously over, but I officially broke things off a couple of days before leaving for home. But before ending things, I did do one more thing. I got petty. I figured since he had wasted my time while claiming to be so busy "working" all summer, the least he could do was cover the rent on my summer share for my last month there. I'm sure he felt guilty for ghosting me after I moved for our relationship, so I told him my job was late paying me and I'd need money for my rent. I was making bank the entire summer so me needing the money was a lie, but I wanted reparations for the way I was treated! I asked for double what I was paying Don to sublet. He turned over the check, and I took Don and myself out to a nice dinner on Randy in addition to paying my last monthly sublet bill. This is before the saved Faith learned the scripture "Vengeance is mine, saith the Lord." I was mad. Try Jesus, but don't try me! Or should I say, the old me. ;-)

What I didn't find out until a year after our breakup was that he had been leading a double life and had a whole other girlfriend! If I deserved some payback before, I was definitely glad I got even a little. Her name was Shannon, and she was interviewed for some local news story, and said, "My boyfriend of two years, Randy..." Wow. This man had been in a relationship with her the *entire* time he was seeing me long distance. I was glad I had the inclination to end it without the proof of the smoking gun.

What's Worse Than a Bad Relationship? Overextending Your Stay in One

Randy apologized profusely, and I tried to move on. The problem was I never cut him off. I continued to allow my whole world to be flipped upside down when he contacted me with the smallest crumbs of attention. When Randy would tell me he and Shannon broke up and that he missed me, I fell for it and would keep hoping he'd show up at my doorstep with roses begging for my forgiveness. After all, people make mistakes, right? Right and wrong. This wasn't just a mistake. It was a calculated, deliberate, premeditated web of lies. That spoke to his character—not just to his bad choices. Randy wasn't interested in committing to me (if he was, he would have done it!), and I was keeping myself from healing. Nearly two years *after* we first broke up, I finally cut off all contact for good. Yes, it took all that time for me to understand I had to draw the line in the sand. I was tired of being strung along and not carrying myself like someone worth the chase.

If you're confused about how someone feels about you, it's not love. If they are ambiguous, it's not love. If they are unclear, it's not love. Stop assembling a team of experts (that is, your girlfriends) every time he sends a text to decode the "real meaning." The real meaning is his lack of real effort. It means it's time to cleanly and quietly exit stage left and cut him off for good.

You don't need to beat yourself up for overextending your stay in a bad relationship. It's very easy to blame yourself, and think "Why was I so stupid?" But you weren't stupid; maybe taken advantage of or naïve about how some people can callously walk through life hurting people who love them, but certainly not stupid. The fact that you walked away is proof of that. Thank goodness you broke up with him and didn't give him another second to hurt you or waste your time!

There are always those "Hallelujah, he's gone" breakups. Sometimes you still love him, even though he drove you crazy. Actually he drove you more than crazy. He drove you through a wall! And it wasn't until it had crashed and gone away that you could go on and heal. If you're reading this and relate, know this: *There's someone else.*

In a different context, those words hit me like a sack of bricks when I first heard them. I was having dinner with a guy friend of mine, Matt, lamenting a breakup I was going through (yes, another one). This was four years after Randy. I was in a happy, committed, healthy relationship with someone whom I thought was amazing—so I thought! I was telling my friend that I was a little confused because I'd been in a great relationship, but my ex was going through some things with his career and told me that he needed space for that and couldn't be in a committed relationship. I respected it and said okay, but at the same time he was still calling me, telling me he missed me, and asking me out to dinner (except not as his girlfriend).

I was so busy fumbling through all the mixed messages I was receiving from this ex that I hadn't realized that I was the only one talking from dinner to dessert. I looked up to see Matt with a sad look on his face. I took a bite of my dessert to allow some air into the room. He didn't rush to say anything to me. He just looked at me while sipping his tea. It was almost as if he didn't want to break the news to me. He had been tasked with popping my bubble and couldn't bear to do it. He'd never had a conversation with my ex, nor had he even ever met him, but he told me in that moment: "Faith, he's met someone else." *What?* I nervously laughed my friend off and let him know that my ex wasn't that kind of guy. We had ended things amicably. I believed him when he said he needed to focus on his professional work.

I'm sure my friend went home that night thinking I would eventually know the truth, and sure enough, I found out later that my ex had in fact met someone else he wanted to date. Oh my gosh, you would have thought someone had told me the most magical place on Earth—Roscoe's Chicken and Waffles—had closed forever. Instead of letting me know, my ex had used work as his scapegoat to end our relationship. I was shocked. My friend knew what was up without having known my ex at all! There was no track record of a wandering eye or any secret strategies to understand why my ex had behaved that way. Somehow my guy friend knew my ex better than I did!

The reason Matt was able to tell me this without hesitation was because he understood men. He understood: men are about action. A man who is ready, willing, and able for a relationship doesn't give up a good woman. A good woman will be an asset to his development. He would have made it work or communicated that he'd be going through a rough patch. But the excuse he gave was just that: an excuse. And I couldn't see it because I wanted to believe he wasn't purely sheltering my feelings.

There is nothing quite as frustrating in a relationship as not knowing where you fit into someone's life. But here is the key to clarity: when their words and actions don't match, the mismatch is where the truth lies. It tells you there is something they're not telling you about how they feel.

What many of us do is demand an answer in the form of "I need to know where I stand," or we insist on a conversation for "closure." As I mentioned earlier, not knowing where you stand tells you where you stand. There are times when you want to talk it out and you want to fill in the gaps, but you don't need that. The fact that there are gaps is enough alone for you to know the answer. Sis, he may very well have been interested in or loved you. But he was not interested enough. Not at this time, anyway. You forcing it wasn't going to help. You don't have to convince a man who is ready, willing, able, and available for a relationship with you to give you clarity on where you stand.

If you're reading this book, you're likely single or trying to learn how to have an authentic love relationship. I'm proud to be a part of your journey and trust that you'll get through this. I don't think a book that addresses relationships could overlook that middle point of being single while still having feelings for a man who is yours no more. The next step after identifying and being honest with yourself that the relationship is over is knowing that you are worthy of more than that. It all falls back on the fact that, as you are growing and developing into a better person, you attract better into your life. Becoming better means valuing yourself enough to recognize that crumbs of attention aren't enough for you.

When Demetrius, the aforementioned ex (who told me he needed to focus on his career), and I were together, we were both deep into our careers and at a more mature stage of being in a relationship. I literally was anticipating a proposal in the coming months, but instead he broke up with me abruptly, claiming things were getting hectic at work. I was blindsided. I cried myself to sleep that night.

After coming out of this fog a few days later, I reminded myself that if he couldn't balance a thriving career with a loving relationship, then he wasn't right for me. Again, though, I was dealing with betrayal. I wanted to be grateful that he had broken up with me instead of cheating on me like Randy had, but the fact that he couldn't be honest with me strengthened my resolve that Demetrius wasn't the man for me.

Little did I know that one year later, he'd be back on my doorstep trying to get back together. Unfortunately for him, I valued myself enough to know not to let him back in. You don't have to be beholden to anyone's apologies. They should treat you right the first time, because you can't guarantee there will be a next time. People who aren't afraid to lose you should not be shocked when you aren't afraid to walk away. I wasn't always this resilient or strong. But over time, having learned the hard way what didn't work, I knew it was time to apply the principles that would serve my well-being. I picked up trade tools for handling breakups with grace until I found my guy.

How to End a Relationship: A Blueprint

I get many questions from women on exactly how to cut off a well-and-done relationship. It's amazing how we spend so much time questioning and pondering our ability to put an end to something that we don't want anymore. I've heard women tell me it took them an entire year to break up with someone, and I don't want that for you. I've put together a blueprint or checklist on how to handle it, particularly if you're on the receiving end. I present to you the Six Guiding Principles of Breakups.

1. DETACH AND LET GO.

When Demetrius told me he could no longer be in a relationship, as much as it hurt, I didn't fight it. I simply said okay, even though

I was absolutely hurt by it. We didn't communicate for a week. The next thing I knew, I was sitting at work one day and he sent me a text, " just checking on you." By me not having a super emotional response (that he knew of) and also not reaching out, he became curious. He started thinking about me more. He thought I was going to resist and make the breakup conversation difficult for him, and when I didn't, he really didn't know what to think.

When a man is moving away from your relationship, the more you try to pull him toward you, the more he will likely repel. The biggest bubble burster in the world is if they say they want to break up, and you agree with it. If they say they need space, agree with it. Say, "I understand," and let go. What if you don't want the breakup to happen? That's fine, but this is the time to hit folks with the plot twist. For whatever reason, this person has chosen to back away from you. When you open up and allow space, you immediately stop pushing them away. The biggest problem people face when it gets to this breakup stage is that they naturally fight against this space. Too often we are stuck in our head trying to justify why we should have control over what's happening. And we look for every logical reason to fight against it. If they want to leave, you must let them walk away in peace. Stop fighting it. Go with the flow. What happens then? He starts wondering why you're not having an emotional reaction. (Cry a river to your BFF but not to him!) He was expecting one and didn't get it. He starts questioning whether he made the right decision because you appear to have it all together. Inevitably, what happens is they get curious, and I can almost guarantee you they'll reach back out to you within a couple months at the latest.

Carl: Hey.
Shantell: Hi.
Carl: Are you mad at me?

Shantell: No. Should I be?

Carl: Well, I figured since the breakup you might be.

Shantell: No, you needed space and I respect that. I wish you well.

Carl: Well, I was just thinking about you and wanted to say hello.

Shantell: K. Bye.

His last text almost took Shantell out, but she remained strong! If Carl wants to come back to the relationship, he can't do it under the guise of friendship. This is the time for her to guard her own heart. He's obviously missing her and checking in to check the temperature. Shantell kept it short and sweet. (It's great to stay sweet; I mean why would you be mad? It's his loss.) Be careful of these checking-in texts—it's low, minimal effort, and often they are a way to keep tabs on you while he is off doing whatever it is he wants. Sometimes you really have to do the cold turkey cutoff.

In the end when a breakup occurs, one of only two things will happen: One, you're out of a relationship with someone who doesn't want it anymore. Everyone has free will. It's okay. That just means there's someone out there who is more compatible with you. Or two, they will recognize the error of their ways and come back. Then it's up to you to decide whether it's worth a second chance.

After a breakup your brain tends to focus on the happy times you had with that person. We fear the loss. So you have to flip that switch in your head. Instead of focusing on the happy times, look at the reasons the relationship ended. This allows you to see with clearer eyes, detach from the person, and face the reality of what's happening. It's all a part of the process of letting go. If they are the one who ended the relationship, letting go will actually give them the space to come back into your life if that's what they desire. Then you get to decide if that's what you want. As you're processing all of this, ask yourself this question: do you really want the relationship, or do you just want to win? If you ended the relationship, detaching and letting go will still allow both of you some much-needed time to process the immediate aftermath of feelings you both have. It's never easy, but this process is necessary to your healing.

Demetrius started asking to see me a week after he ended the relationship. I didn't know about the other woman at the time, but it just didn't sit right with me. Why did my ex want to date me with no commitment? I refused to do it. Best decision I ever made—the only reason he wanted to date me was to have his cake and eat it too. For him, the bakery was closed.

2. UNDERSTAND THE POWER OF NOW.

Being in the now entails focusing on everything we are grateful for in this moment. This especially matters post-breakup. Take a deep breath right now and exhale. What are you grateful for? If you are reading this, you are alive and you are here. When you are present in the moment, you realize this moment is the only moment that matters. This is the only moment that determines our past and creates our future. What you focus on will expand in your life in this moment. What you don't focus on slowly goes away. As long as we keep bringing ourself into the moment and choose loving thoughts for ourself in the moment, we will naturally create peaceful moments. After a breakup, you will probably have more free time. Use it to dream new dreams. Set new goals. Decide to take some classes you've always wanted to take, work out every day, write out positive affirmations. Do everything you can to make your *now* feel good and serve your well-being.

3. DECLINE THE FRIENDSHIP REQUEST (FOR NOW).

When you're going through a breakup is not the time for friendship with your ex. It's not real. Give yourself some time to process what's happened. Many relationship experts agree that for at least thirty days you should take some time off from being in contact, because you need this time to refocus and realign yourself. If you are on the receiving end of the breakup, your ex will likely try to communicate with you or even ask to see you during this time frame. Why? Because you've created space for them and they've started to think about you. Even if they don't want the relationship, your absence in their life is palpable if you haven't been chasing them. To alleviate this uncomfortable space, sometimes one of you will offer friendship. Don't do it. Not at this time.

About that Friend Request

In your desperation, you offer (or accept) friendship because you think if you can just stay in there, even if it's at a downgraded level, your heartbreak will hurt less, or it will be easier to get back together. It makes you feel better because you aren't removed from their life completely. Others think if you can somehow keep yourself in the forefront of their mind and show them what a good person you are or how fly you look, they will fall in love with you again. It doesn't work that way. With friendship, you are put in backup-plan mode. Usually exes offer friendship for one of two reasons:

1. They feel bad for breaking up with you, so it appeases their conscience or guilt.
2. They want to keep you around as an option.

Through the guise of friendship, they can keep tabs on you if you're moving on and then use this intel to try to pull you back in. They aren't ready to let go—all the way—so they offer crumbs. They aren't 100 percent sure about the end of the relationship (usually no one is), but this allows them to keep the door open in case they change their mind. You must reject the offer of friendship. If you think the relationship is worth salvaging, you can say: "I appreciate you wanting to stay in touch as friends, but I don't think that's a good idea right now. If you change your mind about our relationship, then maybe we can talk, but otherwise I wish you the best."

Be polite. And move on.

If you, in fact, want a clean break, you should say that: "I think right now a clean break is best."

Again, be polite and keep it moving.

Let people experience the consequences of breaking up with you. Let them miss you. What will happen is your value will actually rise in their eyes again. If a breakup happened, then somehow that value had been lowered. When they don't see you upset, angry, emotional, begging, they become curious. If you let them take the break they've asked for and give them space—more than they thought, more than they even wanted—it causes them to think, why isn't she being emotional about this? Why isn't she upset? Am I that easy for her to get over? They can't do that if you stay right in the mix trying to convince them not to end the relationship. If you don't cause drama and awkwardness in a breakup, it shows class and maturity. And that's what they will remember you for. They will then reflect on the relationship and the good times. So show strength from the first moment it happens. It's all going to work out for you.

4. IF HE GOES LOW, DON'T GO LOWER.

I was fresh out of law school and ready to put my investigative skills to the test. I suspected Randy (whom we discussed earlier in this chapter) was cheating and it was the end for us—I didn't catch him red-handed, but I could tell he was distancing himself from our relationship. He'd stopped calling regularly. I was seeing him even less. And his excuses weren't adding up. I sat with the feeling at first, but when I eventually brought it up to him, he denied everything. That gut feeling never went away, and I knew in my heart there was someone else. It started to make me feel a bit crazy because here I was convinced something was off, and yet here was my man telling me it was all in my head. Ladies, this right here is called gaslighting, and it's a common tactic for those who know they've done wrong but want to put the emotional burden on you.

The thing about a gut feeling is that just because you're suppressing it doesn't mean it will go away. It continued to gnaw at me until I decided I just *had* to get some proof for the sake of "closure." (Remember how I said closure can be the devil.) In my defense, this was before I became enlightened about life and love, y'all. One day, while he was out of town, I slipped into his New York apartment for some snooping. What started as a quick trip to look around quickly turned into a full on search-and-seizure. I looked high and low! Among other things, I found our couples photos buried in a drawer underneath clothes. I knew I had enough evidence to end the relationship, but the last thing my search provided me with was closure. If anything, it opened a Pandora's box of my emotions.

In the end, I felt like I had taken the low road instead of the high. I had stayed somewhere I wasn't being cherished, and I did so in spite of knowing deep down that the relationship wasn't serving me. My girlfriends later tried to encourage me that I had done what I needed to do in order to leave with a clear conscience—but had I? If I hadn't found what I was looking for that evening, the relationship itself wouldn't have reassured me, so what was the proof really for?

It became clear that I was looking to validate my feelings when they were already valid to begin with. My unhappiness and his actions were enough to realize it wasn't working out. Snooping through his apartment was like pouring salt and lemon juice on my wound. It wasn't going to help me heal from the breakup. I had succeeded in one thing, and that was allowing myself to be brought down to his level, and by not listening to my inner voice and taking his actions for what they were.

I can't control what others do. So what's really left up to me? How I choose to respond. Hiding behind the need for proof is our way of delaying the inevitable. Instead of taking control of the relationship's end, we shift responsibility to the evidence-bearer. In my opinion, this buys us time to keep from facing reality when it could be much simpler to rip the Band-Aid off. I learned from that moment on how to end things cleanly, but I still had some lessons to learn about trusting those gut feelings that every woman has. When you feel at your wit's end, pause for clarity and make sure you leave no room for regret. Betrayal is one thing. Embarrassing yourself by stooping to his level is another.

5. YOU CAN CRY IF YOU WANT TO.

Depending on how and why the relationship ended, you may have some deep emotions to work through. Let it out, even if that means crying yourself to sleep a few nights. But when you wake up in the morning, allow it to be a fresh, calming start. Visualize yourself happy and feel the emotions. And then get on with your day. Set those intentions first thing in the morning and right before you go to bed. Avoid negative and toxic emotions regarding the breakup. Hate has to go. Anger has to go. Frustration, jealousy, envy—they all have to go. These are toxic, low-energy emotions that bring you down. If their social media is upsetting you, stop looking at it. Give yourself those thirty days to clear your mind. Get all the tears out, but then be adamant about focusing on everything you can do to show love to yourself. Go for walks, read inspirational material, listen to uplifting music, go to therapy for a few sessions if you need to. And feel free to cry some more, do whatever you need. Grieving a relationship is natural, and you shouldn't feel bad about it or that you're not being strong. It's best to acknowledge your grief rather than bury it and let it fester into negative behavior or thoughts toward future partners. But then decide, it's time to move forward.

6. BE STILL–DON'T FIGHT FOR THE RELATIONSHIP.

You may say you want to fight for the relationship because you love them. Is your love for someone contingent upon you having a relationship with that person? If you really love someone, don't you want the best for them? When a breakup happens, why then would you want to see them continue to be in a relationship they don't want to be in? If you're having a lot of problems in your relationship but fighting to hold on to it, is it possible that it's actually a selfish act because you want to hold them in an unhappy relationship? Most people just want to hold on to their exes because of ego. Some people just want to win. Whether it's ego, attachment, familiarity, or control—let it go. You will be fine. How do I know? Because you've survived every other challenging day in your life, and you'll survive this one too. Don't think that if you don't have that person in your life anymore, you won't be happy. It simply is not true.

Don't ever attach your happiness to a specific person, place, job, or thing. Because when these things change (and they will), you lose control. Always know your happiness is an inside job, and protect your peace of mind.

If you still love your ex, you have to be big enough to let them go if they want to go. Set them free. Give them the gift of goodbye. I always think nature is the best indicator of how life is: there are no storms that last forever. Just as the seasons come and go, this too shall pass. When we know we are in the divine flow of life, we don't fight against the current. We need to learn to trust and totally surrender ourselves into the hands of divine timing. Who are we not to trust life's timing?

When you let go, one of two things will likely happen:

1. The person either comes back, as we discussed (and you decide whether the relationship is best for you); or
2. You realize there is something or someone out there that is better for you.

Either way, operate from a position of strength and love. This will allow you to process things from a clear space. Set your intentions to be grateful for the way in which you will grow from this experience. Tell yourself: there is a lesson in this for me. Pain is inevitable, but suffering is optional. Write it down. *What is the lesson?*

When you're in the middle of a painful situation, ask yourself these critical questions:

1. What does this situation say about the other people involved? One of my favorite books for understanding human nature is *The Four Agreements,* and one of the biggest lessons from the book is to take nothing personally, because nothing others do is because of you.
2. What red flags may I have missed? How can I identify those earlier on to avoid this pain in the future?
3. What else is there for me to learn here?

The key to breaking up properly is not overextending your stay in a broken relationship. Process your emotions, explore the lesson, but make a clean exit from the relationship. Your ex may want to keep you in the sunken place. Remember in the film *Get Out,* when the main character gets put into a trance, leaving him in the "sunken place"? The sunken place is no control over your body or actions, you're just stuck! It feels like walking in the wrong direction on an escalator. You're rationing out your time, affection, and in some cases, even your cookie, for ambiguity. Cut that off. Make it done, in full. This goes for those exiting a fairly new relationship, a long-term one, or if you're a divorced bae. Note to divorcees: Do not hold on to a relationship that was legally pronounced "done." Even if you have children with your ex, establish boundaries. I'm all for coparenting, but are you inviting your ex to the zoo with the kids for their well-being or for your own comfort? Know this difference. Let go of the worn past. Create real structure and boundaries if you're co-parenting or are required to see your ex often, as in cases like having a business together. Make room for newness on your path. When life is throwing you signs and a man is telling you with his actions (or legal documents) that it's over, don't make him repeat himself. You deserve love, autonomy, and to be with someone who you know values you. As our Queen Mother Angela Bassett shouted in *Black Panther*, "Show them who you are!"

Reclaiming Your Time

You determine your worth, and so the goal in moving on from a breakup is knowing how much you are willing to walk away from that which doesn't serve you. How many times have you fought for a relationship that you know wasn't healthy just because "hey—at least it was something!"? If you stand for nothing, you'll fall for anything, and this definitely applies to your romantic life. Non-negotiables are just that—non-negotiable. There should be no amount of sweet talking that can talk you away from giving yourself everything you need and deserve now. In *Men Are from Mars, Women Are from Venus*, John Gray suggests that women have a need to feel special while men have a need for peace and respect. Men want peace and respect. We may throw some other desires and life plans into the mix, but this is what it boils down to.

Like a big puzzle, each piece fits somewhere perfectly. When we try to force it, we leave ourselves depleted and devalued. Oftentimes people stay in bad situations in fear that there won't be anything better. We are surrounded by people telling us that love is "hard" and that sometimes this is as good as it's going to get. *Never* feed into that fear. There will always be something better...even if that something is *not* being in this *bad* situation. You'll realize while walking away from half-baked love that it's a waste of your time. Imagine an undone cake. Any baker will tell you what that means: either you didn't put the right ingredients in for it to rise to its full potential or you moved too fast and took it out of the oven when it wasn't ready. Like love, baking a cake takes several steps and lots of patience. Don't sacrifice quality.

It's possible to be genuinely happy in life and in love. Daily joy, getting what our heart desires, securing our life's dreams is possible for you and me. How do you make a fresh start? Accept that what happened in your past does not have to spill over to the freshness of this new day. Choose different thoughts for a different path.

Women are nurturers by nature, and we love hard! Now I have to keep it real: sometimes that means we do "a lot" and go 0 to 100 real quick. But it's because, on a primal level, we crave companionship, security, and happiness...and we want it now, as we should. When we see a man whom we feel represents that, we dive right in. There's nothing wrong with that; just make sure the next man you're head over heels for is actually adding those things to your life!

What I want you to deeply understand henceforth is that when you're with a man who is good for your soul, you'll feel safe and more secure. If the one you're with doesn't bring that to the table, what are you there for?

Chapter 12

Forgiveness Is Closure: Case Closed

"Today I decided to forgive you...
because my soul deserves peace."

—NAJWA ZEBIAN

If you're like me, you have some Oprah quotes in your arsenal that you live by. One of mine is, "True forgiveness is when you can say, thank you for that experience." Forgiveness saved my life time and time again without me truly realizing it. When I was being dragged down by ambivalent men and mixed signals, forgiveness threw me a life vest and helped me learn to swim again. And if you're thinking, *That's too passive for me, Faith; I'm more of a revenge girl*, trust me, a lot of us have once thought the same. You may encounter the worst of the worst, but you know what could be worse? You could be them. But you're not. Don't let any of your exes turn you into something you're not.

But that doesn't mean it is always easy to turn the other cheek! Judge shows are popular because people like to see justice get served, so I'm no stranger to seeing retribution. As we go through life—it doesn't matter how smart, rich, or privileged you are— everyone is susceptible to being treated unfairly. It's the same with love. I've seen many litigants who have been swindled by charismatic manipulators, taken advantage of, abused, harassed, or just plain cheated. They've tried everything to come to a resolution, and my courtroom is their last stop to get their grievances heard. With families and exes, in particular, I deal with the legal aspect of the case, but what's far more damaging is what's often left unresolved: the emotional complexities of hurt, anger, and resentment.

When I was an assistant district attorney in Manhattan, handling criminal cases, innocent victims often asked variations of the same question: "Why did this have to happen to me?" or "What did I do to deserve this?" Victims often think that conviction brings closure. It helps them to pick up the pieces and allows them to move on. Criminal convictions can provide closure in a legal sense, but rarely in an emotional sense. What I see far too often is even after victims win the battle in court, they've lost the war in their minds. They struggle daily to move past how they've been aggrieved. Long after the perpetrator has had any direct role in their life, they continue to point the finger at them.

In instances of betrayal or pain at the hands of a lover or in a relationship, I'll be honest with you, sis, many don't bounce back. I want more for you than to live like that. It's no way to live if you're holding on to the pain and trauma of a past relationship or breakup. Some unhealthy habits of the brokenhearted are that they don't just blame that person for a past event that hurt them, they continue to blame them for current failures and life experiences. As a result, instead of whatever injustice they've experienced being relegated to the past, they carry the mantle of hurt into their future relationships. One of the most important lessons you can learn is how to cope after a painful relationship or broken heart—and how important forgiveness is in your path to healing. Even if you're not currently suffering, most of us have had our hearts broken. I think you can tell by my stories that I have. And "broken" can be an understatement of what some of us have gone through. "Smashed," "shattered," "dragged" are more fitting words for some. That's why when thinking ahead about the relationship that you want, it's important to take care of the baggage. The past is the past, and you're making a decision to move on without looking back. It's a process, and you may have to make that decision time and again, but every time you do, it gets easier. Once you get to that place, finding new love will be a lot more joyful and fulfilling, and most important, you'll feel the happiness you deserve.

Healing Through Disrespect

No one knows the pain of betrayal better than my friend Marshawn Evans. Marshawn is every man's dream woman—highly accomplished, beautiful, talented, smart, and fun. Committed to her faith, she even remained celibate waiting for her wedding night. In her circle of friends, she did everything right, so of course she would meet her prince charming, fall in love, and live happily ever after. In the midst of planning her dream wedding, she endured a stunning betrayal that shocked everyone in her world—including her.

Marshawn and I met when I was Miss Louisiana and she was competing for Miss Texas. Later, she attended Georgetown University School of Law, won the title of Miss DC, and became third runner-up to Miss America. Marshawn was always so sweet, smart, and deserving, so I was thrilled when her boyfriend, a divorced father of two, proposed to her. But a few days before their big Atlanta wedding, the bridegroom's ex-wife sent Marshawn an email detailing an affair they were having. She alleged it had been going on the entire time Marshawn and her fiancé had been dating. She told Marshawn she waited until he was getting on the plane for their Atlanta wedding before revealing the affair because she wanted to maximize the hurt and embarrassment. Marshawn didn't believe her. She wanted proof. Marshawn picked up the phone and called the ex-wife. The woman proceeded to describe Marshawn's bedroom and bathroom in detail. She had indeed been in her home. Marshawn called her fiancé, and he repeatedly denied the affair. She waited to pick him up from the airport in Atlanta, and when she saw his face at baggage claim, she instantly knew he had been lying. By this time all of her family and friends were on their way to Atlanta. Reality was setting in: the entire time Marshawn had been in this committed relationship—waiting until their wedding night to have sex—her man was sleeping with his ex-wife. Marshawn called off the wedding a few days before the ceremony.

Can you imagine the agony of the betrayal, and then having to tell all her friends and family who'd just arrived in town to celebrate "the happiest day of her life" about it? How do you recover after that? How do you trust again? How do you move on? Well, she did, beautifully. First, she grieved the relationship. Like I said before, it's okay to be sad about the end of the dream. It was not an easy time for her. The healing process is just that—a process. It can be uncomfortable and hard. She may have had her heart broken, but she was not broken. Then, she dreamed a new dream. She knew she had to pick up the pieces.

Second, she understood that the rejection of this marriage was redirection in her life. Imagine if she had married someone who was capable of such lies and deceit. His ex-wife did her a favor! She had in actuality dodged a bullet. Third, she had to release the anger and resentment. She didn't want her heart to harden and push love away. She used her faith to believe that the best was still yet to come in her life. Lastly, she let go of the man and the relationship. Sometimes it felt impossible that she would ever get over him. But she did.

Marshawn worked through the pain of that betrayal so she could open her heart to a new man. If you've been betrayed, it's only natural to be suspicious, waiting for the shoe to drop in your next relationship. But that's not learning from your experiences, it's reliving them. To go forward, you have to close that chapter of your life titled *A Woman Betrayed* and write a new one called *Bliss Is Mine*. Make peace with your past, enjoy the present, have hope for the future. In a world where so many people take action based on their fears—fear of getting hurt again, fear of failure, fear of rejection—make a point to be driven by your dreams. That's all you need to remember.

Marshawn is now married to the man of her dreams, has her own business, and wrote a book about resilience titled *Believe Bigger*. When she met her now husband, she shared her story, and together they worked through how she could learn to build trust in him. And she did. She didn't make him pay for what someone else had done. They are now the parents of triplet girls! Marshawn tells her story to inspire women all over the world that there is hope after being hurt. You have to be willing to pick up the pieces and keep going.

As for the ex-wife, the great philosopher Confucius said, "Before you embark on a journey of revenge, dig two graves." In the quest to destroy another person, you also destroy yourself. What you give out in life is bound to return.

Release Them

My bench on TV is a civil court, not criminal, but many couples come in carrying grudges as big, old, and set in stone as Mount Rushmore. One couple, the modern Hatfields and McCoys, had been going back and forth at each other for five years over what started out as a minor fender bender. Another case between ex-lovers was so dramatic, with so many twists and turns, we needed two episodes to do it justice. The woman was a few months pregnant. Her ex-boyfriend believed she got pregnant on purpose and refused to accept that the baby was his.

We had to go through a series of acrimonious disputes, and the testimony of his new fiancée (yes, already). The big finale of the case was my revealing the results of a DNA paternity test he'd agreed to take. It came back positive. He was, with 99.99 percent certainty, the father. If he wanted to be in his child's life—he said he did—they were both going to have to put down their grudges. Even if the woman did get pregnant on purpose, he had to let it go. Even if he did sleep with her while he was newly engaged to another woman, she had to get past it. Otherwise, they'd pass their rage at each other down to their child. That's not an inheritance that anyone needs or wants.

No one ever dies from a snake bite alone. It's the venom that continues to pour through your system after the bite that kills. The same goes for holding onto grudges. It's the built-up anger and resentment continuing to occupy your mind that ends up destroying your spirit and your future relationships. Anger is not happening to you. It's happening within you—if you allow it. The ball is in your court; the moment you know something is no longer serving, you then pass it.

When you can stop justifying the reasons you continue to hold court in your mind with an ex, then you take away their power and own that space in your head again. Tell yourself: no one has the power to make me feel any kind of way without my consent. When you take responsibility for how you feel, you have the ability to fix things when you don't feel good. When blame goes, the game is over. And you win.

When someone hurts you, you may feel debilitated. You can't eat. You can't sleep. You can't work. It can impact every area of your life. The feeling of a broken heart can be devastating. The old saying that time will heal these wounds is simply not true. There are many adults today who still struggle with anger and resentment from painful events in their childhood. So how are they supposed to heal from a relationship that just ended last month? There are people who go from one relationship to the next, continuing to carry trauma from their past. Sometimes it's easier not to have to face what's really hurting on the inside. But it is worth it. It takes time, effort, and a decision to forgive. It's a process. Time doesn't heal wounds—but in many cases, it reveals them.

If left unaddressed, life's circumstances will trigger the very things you once thought you had gotten past. Healing from past hurt begins with you. It takes time and intentional effort. It doesn't just happen, especially if your conception of healing looks like listening to heartbreak music and fantasizing about revenge. Forgiveness is a matter of your will. Your past experiences of hurt are now a thought and a feeling you carry around. Left unaddressed, these thoughts build into anger. The anger builds into resentment. And the resentment builds into hate. All of these represent deadly emotions and energy-stunting feelings that disempower you as you continue to let them occupy space in your mind. You must release them on your path to healing. The only time that matters in this scenario is your decision to do these things right now.

Affirmations for Becoming a Better You

Repeat after me:

1. I am strong. Weeping may endure for a night, but joy comes in the morning! (Psalm 30:5). Through my resilience, I create a joyful future.
2. I am confident. I accept things I can't change, have courage to change the things I can, and possess the wisdom to know the difference.
3. I am at peace. I am like a bottle of water, not a can of soda. When shaken, a can of soda will open and explode, but no matter what, like water, I will remain still.
4. I am enough. And that's on everything.

Todd, a recent divorcé, and Christie, who'd never been married, met on a dating app where the women were required to initiate contact. She swiped on Todd's profile and sent him a heart message. The two exchanged a series of messages before they decided to meet up. They started talking and thought they had a lot in common. Todd pursued Christie hard—called her every day. Sent her check-in texts. Took her out to nice dinners and occasionally sent her flowers. They fell in love quickly. Christie thought she had a wonderful relationship with a man who said he wanted to marry her within the first three months of them dating. He *did* adore her, but she started to notice he had a lot of female friends whom he seemed hesitant to introduce her to. He would go through an attractive woman's social media page and "like" all of her photos (huge red flag to Christie).

When she was traveling for work, he and a female friend went to the movies, and the woman posted a photo of them together. He said it was innocent, and it probably was. But Christie thought his need to hang out with all these single women was concerning (she'd lost track of red flags by now).

After several conversations around the subject, Todd told Christie that these women were all just friends. Given that Todd's recent marriage had ended because of his infidelity, Christie decided she wasn't comfortable with Todd's lack of boundaries and with the fact that he didn't want to introduce these women to her. For a few months, she was admittedly torn over whether it was the right decision. She told me that he tried so hard to be a good boyfriend, but it was just his nature to put himself out there as a Casanova. They kept in touch for months, but then she realized he was causing her more pain during their breakup than even when they were together. He was going out of his way to flaunt other women on social media while still telling her he loved her. In an effort to make her jealous, he was pushing her further away. But still, Christie held out hope that he would get his act right, because they did have some happy times together.

It all came to a head on Christmas. He posted a photo of a line of Christmas stockings, one with his name, ones with names of other members of his family, and one with the name of another woman he'd been dating after the two of them broke up. He included her in a sweet family photo that he'd put online for the world—including Christie—to see.

Christie finally became clear about her decision: this couldn't possibly be love. Love didn't seek to hurt and humiliate. After the pictures, what Christie was once on the fence about she was now certain of. It was over. She deserved so much better than a man who would continually flaunt other women in front of her. So she cut him off for good.

Todd still wanted to stay friends. As I explained earlier, sometimes friendship is appropriate with the passage of time. But what Todd wanted—this faux friendship for the sake of having contact with Christie—was a big no-no. Ladies, beyond that, there's a lesson here about healing: how people treat you when your relationship is going through difficulty matters. Don't excuse cruel, insensitive behavior—adversity reveals the true person. If they didn't have cruelness inside of them, it wouldn't come out of them.

One of the hardest things you will ever do is grieve the loss of a person who's still alive, especially when he's posting photos of himself on Instagram at parties, laughing with his arms around other women. You might start posting your own "over it!" staged photos. This is not healing. It's posturing. If that's happening, I recommend unfriending and unfollowing your ex—and key mutual friends—at least for the time being. Some might call this rash or weak; I call it self-compassion. Yes, you want to reach a stage of enlightenment where you are unbothered by anything your ex is doing. But until you get there, your job is to protect your peace. Unfollow, sis.

Compartmentalizing is good! Distraction combats stress, and if you keep yourself busy, you can get a heck of a lot done. After one breakup, I threw myself into work. To burn bright, I said yes to every media appearance and event offer I could. All those on-air segments were noticed by a man named Hank Cohen, the CEO of Trifecta Entertainment. He wrote me an email that said he'd seen me on Bill O'Reilly's show on Fox one night and with Al Sharpton on MSNBC the next. If I could handle those polar opposite audiences and hosts on consecutive nights, he believed, I had broad appeal, and he wanted to talk about my hosting a court show.

I did some research on him and his production company, decided he seemed legit, and got in touch. Soon after, we shot a pilot for *Judge Faith*. I lost a boyfriend but gained a TV show. A better than fair trade. And guess what? That show has outlasted the doomed relationship and changed my life forever.

A favorite quote of mine from the poet Mark Anthony is, "And one day she discovered that she was fierce, and strong and full of fire, and that even she couldn't hold herself back because her passion burned brighter than her fears."

Who Are You Renting To? The Past or Your Peace

According to the Merriam-Webster dictionary, forgiveness is the act of giving up any thought of harm or revenge even when it might be justified. And that's where the work comes in. Forgiveness is an action to protect your own mental health. It's about releasing the ties that keep you emotionally engaged with the injustice you experienced.

Motivational speaker Dr. Michael Beckwith says in his book that if you're carrying un-forgiveness, the message you are telling yourself is "someone owes me something."

I'd also like to add to Beckwith's analysis that unforgiveness also is another form of "I'm missing something" and "I don't have something."

Take back your power.

When you choose forgiveness, you reclaim your own power. You learn to make peace with the fact that there is an outstanding debt from someone that can't be repaid. You learn to accept an apology you never received. You learn to deal with life when it turns out differently from what you wanted without staying bitter.

Forgiveness begins with a decision to release yourself from being beholden to the past regardless of what anyone has said or done. By changing the way you choose to perceive the power that others have over you, you empower yourself to be able to let go of anything.

My parents grew up in the South during the era of Jim Crow. These laws were put into place to keep Black people separate from whites in public spaces. Water fountains were designated "white only." For Black folks, someone else was deciding what water fountains we could drink out of. Someone else was deciding where we could sit in a restaurant. Someone else was deciding where we could rest our weary feet on public transportation. It was an explicit form of bondage.

In a similar and less systemic way, deciding whether you're happy or unhappy based on someone else's actions or behaviors—it's an insidious form of bondage. Because if someone else has to change or do something different in order for you to be happy, you have just given your power away. When you retain that power—the choice is solely yours—that's liberating! We have to fight to reclaim our power over our own disposition and reactions. We can't control how others handle or treat us, but we have complete control of how we respond.

Emotions are real but they can also be volatile. Your happiness is not contingent on any one person. In the case of one couple I came across, this lesson was learned the hard way. Janae and Jaden worked together and were keeping things quiet because of that. They had been successful at dating in secret for a few months, when he made the choice to end things. There was no cheating or grandiose excuse—he simply wasn't very happy and had made a decision to end the relationship. Unfortunately, the young woman he had just left heartbroken wouldn't accept that. In fact, she told him that he "couldn't" break up with her and tried to physically keep him from leaving the apartment!

Her immediate response was an act of desperation and self-preservation. She held onto him while crying and arguing with him about how wrong he was. She cried that she couldn't survive life without him. She had a successful career, so he wasn't financially supporting her. They'd never gone public with the relationship, so there was even less to explain to folks. What it really boiled down to was that her self-worth had become tied to her relationship with this man. She saw her life flash before her eyes when he decided to end the relationship, and it triggered desperate behavior. No one is immune to the sense of loss you can feel in the aftermath of a breakup. But we must learn to separate these *feelings* from the *facts*.

Feeling: *I can't get over this.*
Fact: You can and you will.

Feeling: *I can't live without him.*
Fact: Yes, you can. You will go to sleep and wake up the next morning living and breathing at the start of a brand new day.

Feeling: *I won't ever be as happy.*
Fact: Actually, you will! You are resilient, beautiful, and worthy of the life ahead of you.

Sometimes we hold onto the pain or anger because we get

comfortable in victimhood. You are the CEO of your mind, and no one else can choose how you feel, except for you. You're the only one who controls what you allow in. Relinquishing that control anywhere else—whether toward loving or loathing—is a form of bondage.

Chicago-Sun Times advice columnist Ann Landers famously said, "Hanging onto resentment is letting someone you despise live rent-free in your head." Would you ever let someone you despise live rent-free in your home? Absolutely not. So why are you allowing them to live rent-free in your head? Because this is exactly what happens with your mind when you harbor grievances. You give these energy-draining thoughts a space to live and thrive at your expense. You feed them energetically and shelter them emotionally.

In Dr. Fred Luskin's book *Forgive for Good*, the transpersonal psychologist explains that a grievance occurs when:

- Something happens in life that we didn't want to happen.
- We deal with the problem by thinking about it too much.

When these two things happen simultaneously, we basically rent out too much space in our minds to that particular hurt.

When the majority of your thoughts come from a place of anger, resentment, and fear, that's what you will continue to see manifest in your life.

I have people who claim they don't like me or my show, but they still follow me on social media. Anytime I post, they express their dislike! It always baffles me why they would continue to go somewhere that upsets them. Who knows something upsets them, yet seeks it out further, and signs up for post notifications to be alerted about their presence? That's like going over to your neighbor's house every day, knocking on their door just to tell them to kick rocks. That's a waste of time and energy. Well, over-thinking to the point of obsession is on a similar level! Stop going out of your way to stay fixated on your frustrations. Wallowing in your anger or sadness is the definition of "misery likes company." Don't allow yourself to stay stuck in time because your mind and heart won't let go.

When a relationship turns out differently than you expected, you may feel you've experienced an injustice. Your truth is valid! However, radical acceptance is when you stop asking why it happened or crying because it did, and get to the good place of *this is the reality of what happened and now I choose to focus on how I will cope.* Coping is a process. It's not one and done after one moment of feeling "I'm over it." In order to truly heal, we have to understand that it may be ongoing. The first thing is to develop habits and practices for coping and acceptance.

Practice Speaking Love into Existence

Take three minutes of quiet time in the morning (or at night) when your mind is quietest. Close your eyes and visualize yourself in the relationship you dream of having. See yourself doing the things you want to do with your partner. See yourself laughing, smiling, and engaging with them. Open your eyes.

Affirm at the end of every sitting: *I now allow myself to have the relationship I desire.*

Now, go about your day, knowing that what you want is on the way.

Just for Me

Please do not use the forgiveness process as an excuse to contact your ex. "Well, Judge Faith told me to forgive, so I decided to call you up and let you know that I'm not mad anymore!" Back away from the phone, my friend. Don't do this, because what you're really looking for is a way to converse again.

Well, contacting him is a part of my closure. Just say you want to contact him—because no one can give you closure. That comes from you. And the last thing you want to do is reach out to someone who doesn't want to hear from you.

About two months after I got engaged, I received a long email from one of my exes. It was all about how sorry he was for the way he treated me and how he hoped I forgave him. Apparently, he was in this process of discovery and healing and wanted to communicate that I'd always have a special place in his heart.

Y'all, I did not need this message of contrition from him. He'd already apologized to me once two years prior; I accepted it then and moved on. Here I was happily engaged and poppin' bottles and he's being Darryl Downer! For whatever reason, because I chose not to be friends with him, he took that to mean I was holding some kind of grudge. Simply not true. Forgiveness does not mean reconciliation. In fact, there are many cases when reconciliation (or any form of contact) is not advisable, such as in cases of domestic abuse, violence, or sexual abuse. Forgiveness is not about letting someone off the hook. You can choose to forgive someone and never speak to them again. You can choose to forgive someone who has never apologized to you. You can choose to forgive someone and still require them to appear in court or face legal consequences for a crime committed against you. Remember those Just for Me perm commercials from back in the day? Get that jingle stuck in your head and remember that forgiveness is for you, not them.

As I said, convictions provide closure in a legal sense, but never in an emotional sense. The emotional healing sought from closure will never come from a judge or jury or the actions of another—it will always come from within. Releasing anger, fear, and resentment is the best way to move forward from pain. It's not for the sake of the perpetrator, but for yourself. It's hard to move forward if you're carrying 2,000 pounds of anger on your shoulders. Shed those unwanted pounds or be crushed by them. Some people think that if you give up on anger, it's a sign of weakness. No. It takes a strong person to forgive. Don't let pain and fury rent space in your head. Get out a figurative broom and sweep it clean, sis.

Every few months, I do a juice cleanse. By eliminating certain foods from my body, I'm eliminating toxins that have built up over time. This gives my digestive system a break and allows it to heal and better absorb nutrients in the future. The goal is to remove the impurities and refuel the body with healthy and nutritional alternatives. After a cleanse, I feel a huge difference in my body—I feel lighter, healthier, and more energetic. A cleanse takes discipline, focus, and determination to see it through. Just as we make the effort to cleanse our bodies of toxins for our physical health, we should do the same with our minds. Good emotional health comes from detoxifying and releasing the residue from hurt that builds up over time. Left unattended, we internalize hurt and allow it to steep into our emotional beings. Emotional detoxes are just as important as physical ones. Give yourself mental wellness check-ins: ask yourself how you're doing. How are you feeling? Are you making good choices to feel good?

And always remember that you can do all of this and still choose not to reconcile with the offending person. There is a gift in goodbye. Remember, your journey to emotional health is the utmost priority.

Your Forgiveness Assignment

Step 1: Reflect...

1. What is a moment in your life that you need to heal from? Describe it.
2. How does this make you feel?
3. What is an important lesson you can learn or take from the experience?
4. Have you grown from it?
5. What actions do you need to take to forgive and move forward?
6. What, if anything, are you grateful for after that experience?
7. When you choose to let go, what opens up for you?

Step 2: Juicing Recipe for Feeling Better from the Inside Out

Painful experiences of any kind can be so depleting that you'll want to replenish your energy levels physically to heal emotionally.

Ingredients

1 bunch curly kale, roughly chopped

1 large lemon, peeled and quartered

1 inch of fresh ginger, peeled

1 large cucumber, cut into strips

2 large Granny Smith apples, cored and sliced

4 whole celery stalks

Instructions

Wash and prep the veggies and fruits.

Juice them in the order listed.

Optional: strain through a sieve (if you don't like pulp).

Drink immediately and enjoy!

Some of us wait too long to acknowledge the pain. Then we don't put enough thought into how exactly to get out of it. Acceptance can sound like something right out of a Tony Robbins speech, but I promise you it will improve your life in every single area if you become what I call "an acceptance practitioner." Acceptance is a mental activity. It's like playing mental jump rope with yourself, but the good news is you're turning in the right direction—soon you will be one with acceptance, and certain stress will be eliminated, fear will seem like an old lover, and you'll find your relationships are filled with much more ease and joy.

To practice acceptance with the one who hurt you, think about it, and yes, I advise you to write it down!

Acceptance is the Holy Grail! It's the initiation into true peace. Peace is the stuff that helps you sleep well at night. Acceptance of exes who mistreated you is the starting point to getting to where you need to be in order to be ready for something more—and wonderful! I know it sounds strange, but acceptance is what you've been looking for in order to get to the next level.

Whether you need to forgive an ex who is an abuser, cheater, or just someone who just flat out stopped loving you, the person (or people) at the helm of these offenses don't deserve your time, energy, or love anymore. We must accept what happened in order to be able to move on fully and in a healthy way. Let go of letting your heart, mind, or any part of you hold on to that experience. It may not be easy, because some of us have been through brutal and serious circumstances. (And it's good to seek therapy for help.) You may be thinking, *That's too much. I forgive them, and now you want me to accept it, Faith?* Yes, because it's not about what they deserve, it's about what *you* deserve. Despite it all, you deserve peace, and accepting what happened is key.

Acceptance means removing all judgment of them or yourself. We make mistakes or bad decisions, but we are not those mistakes or bad decisions. We grow and learn, and there's no shame in any of that! You are a queen—you don't need to harbor any of that in your heart any longer. Start doing the work right now, and watch how you and your relationships begin to transform.

Going forward I want you to think like this: even if he cheated on you, abused your finances, or whatever it was, you are a gladiator in the relationship arena, because everything that happens to you serves as new fuel and strengthens you. Instead of holding on to regret, you ask yourself strengthening questions like *What can I do next time to make things work better for me?*

When many people think of the lesson, they think of what happened at the end. Sis, instead of waiting, suffering, and then learning the lesson later, you can decide to get the lesson now. Yes, while you're in the midst of the difficulty, you can decide to get out in front of it. When you've learned to do this, you've taken the power out of the offense. You now regain home court advantage over yourself. Going forward, you'll continue to win and understand that all endings are new beginnings. The end of a job, a romance, or a friendship sets you on a new path to find another, better one. Case closed.

Too many people go through life looking for reasons to be offended. And that's why consistent forgiveness and acceptance practices are necessary. Case in point: We live in a legalistic society. We have rules for everything. And when these rules aren't met, we learn to address things with sharp comebacks and terse one-liners. We have unrealistic and impossible expectations that people should drive perfectly at the precise speed limit, walk at the right pace, and excuse me, dare they not hold every door open for the next person. People have been killed after being cut off in traffic. What started as a sharp right turn ends in death. A lot of people stand at the ready to tell someone off at the drop of a dime. And when you look for it, you'll find that there is no shortage of people to be mad at. The moral of this is, the world has enough cynics, critics, and naysayers already. Be different. Show and extend grace at every turn, forgive and don't get so mad at others if they don't. I truly believe what you put out into this Earth comes back to you. And when you show grace, when you can recognize someone just might be having a bad day, and refuse not to take everything personally, you win. In life and love, stop projecting impossible rules on the world around you. Make the law of the land love.

In my early twenties, I celebrated my birthday in New York with my long-distance boyfriend at the time. Yes, *that* boyfriend, who was cheating the whole time. We know Randy's bad news now, but in the moment, I still thought he was smart, funny, and charismatic. He was several years older than me and already had a hugely successful career in television. I had dated a few different guys in New York, but this relationship felt the most serious. When he told me that he was planning on proposing, my heart swelled. I could have a wedding and finally a life with the man of my dreams, someone I respected and loved. The feeling was short-lived as I discovered soon after he ghosted me that he was dating someone else. I was strong enough to break it off, but emotionally I was all over the place. I didn't know how to handle it. He wanted to stay in touch, be friends, and occasionally sent me flowers out of guilt.

I allowed him to keep in touch with me, and as result I continued an emotional bond with him that I just couldn't break. I was up and down emotionally even at the sight of an email from him. I had completely relinquished emotional control. I forgave him for cheating, and we were never in a relationship again, but I never held him accountable. He still had access to me. He could call when he wanted to call. He could write when he wanted to write. Even if I was angry in my reply to him, it was communication. One day he said, "You're bitter." As much as I didn't want to believe it, he was right. I had let so much resentment build over time that it had struck a nerve. I'd ruminated on his cheating and replayed it in my mind so much the wound was as fresh as if it had happened yesterday.

Again, you never die from a snake bite. It's the venom that pours through your system afterward. It wasn't his act of cheating that caused bitterness. It was the venom—the thoughts about it for two years—that had taken root. I blamed him for any and all unhappiness I was experiencing in my life. I would go two or three months without talking to him, and then he'd pop up again with an email or call, and it always seemed to shake my world. When I realized how much he controlled my emotions and moods, I knew I had to change. My future husband wasn't going to marry a battered and emotionally traumatized woman, especially not because of this dude.

My healing included learning to accept an apology I would never receive. It also included action: I cut him off completely. Then I started the process of forgiveness; I had to unravel the toxic emotions I'd stored in my mind. I did everything I described in this chapter. I stopped blaming, stopped looking to him for closure, forgave him, and also held him accountable by severing the fake friendship. He simply didn't deserve to have access to me. I did the work. When my husband met me several years later, I was healed, whole, and had spent years filling myself up with love. I could only give love if I had it to share. Only the loving find love. And it certainly found me.

When you make the decision to stop outsourcing your happiness and become more inner-directed, your life will change. People often say: forgive and forget. I don't think it's realistic to tell someone to forget about a hurtful past. But you can choose not to save it or keep reliving it. If you're still struggling as you put yourself on a path to healing, just keep doing the work. Sometimes even pretending to forget gets you to where you want to be on your journey to emotional health. But clap back at any self-resistance to dive in deep to your healing, sis!

Moving Past Petty

Growing up, in church I would hear Sunday school lessons on the importance of forgiveness. But I couldn't ever remember being taught how. I would find myself forgiving someone and being angry again the next day at the very thought of their unfair behavior. I then learned that forgiveness wasn't a one-time event. Often, I had to work on it daily with a specific person until I truly let it go.

Though I've gone into great detail about forgiveness, I know how hard it can be to get there. I once ended a relationship with someone (let's call him Marcus) and stopped communicating with him because I thought it was the best way for me to heal and move forward. Weeks turned into months, and I realized how much anger I harbored toward Marcus. It bothered me that I was randomly thinking about him, and it would shift my entire mood. He could have been minding his business on the golf course and there I was furious at him and the world. I decided for my own mental health, I had to forgive Marcus so that I could regain my peace and hold on to indifference toward him. That would be my true test.

I reminded myself: forgiveness would not be friendship. I had enough real friends, ones who would never intentionally cause me pain. As we discussed, it would not mean reconciliation: I still wouldn't respond to his messages or calls. I knew his efforts to communicate with me were a way for him to try to keep me tied to the relationship. I cut him off completely but still had to do the work for my own emotional health. Also, I never reached out to him for closure. I never told him "I forgive you" because I wasn't doing it for him—I was doing it for me. It was time to stop holding onto the offense and allowing it to occupy the space in my mind. I wrote down on a scrap of paper:

I am here because of the choices I made.
I now choose something different.
Different choices will produce different results.

I took a picture of him as a young boy and put the paper on my bulletin board. Every day when I looked at that bulletin board I would see the face of an innocent child. I was able to empathize with the ten-year-old version of him. Scientists have studied what happens in the brain when we think about forgiving and how empathy plays an important role. Turns out, the ability to empathize with the wrongdoer and emotionally identify with them can be important components of the forgiveness response.

I thought about Marcus's childhood and how we had been raised very differently. I thought about the values that had simply not been instilled in him as a child and how that had carried over into adulthood. I thought about the hurt and pain he'd experienced in his life and how it had impacted him. He tried to be a good man. He fell short, and his actions hurt, but at the end of the day, he couldn't give the love that he never received. Imagining him as an innocent child needing love and support was imperative. This allowed me to recognize him as a vulnerable person who was wounded and who had wounded me in return. The hurt I felt was a result of the hurt he experienced. It didn't excuse his behavior to continue that cycle, but I *was* able to release him from blame.

Empathy was for my wholeness because I wanted to manifest a loving relationship in my life, not more of the hurt he gave me. Only the loving find healthy love. My goal was to shift my dominant thoughts to focusing on unconditional love.

True healing work starts with your thoughts: make a conscious effort to refuse to dwell on negative, harmful thoughts about the person who hurt you. You don't have to think positive thoughts either—you can shift yourself to other thoughts altogether. Second, refrain from speaking negatively about them. Stop replaying the offense to your friends every week. All you're doing is continuing to give it energy. Again, you don't have to say good things. If you refrain from speaking negatively about them, and refrain from ruminating on the offense, it helps reshape the kind of energy you are projecting altogether.

The Forgiveness Pledge

Today I choose to forgive _____. I set them free. I release them from any offensive act committed against me. It is all in the past. I release all of the memories, anger, hurt, and resentment that may be buried in my heart. My heart is healed. My heart is unencumbered. I am whole. I move forward freely now. I choose to focus on thoughts that strengthen me today—thoughts of peace, love, and harmony.

While forgiveness and empathy for an offender are key to healing, so should we shower the same kindness on ourselves. In self-forgiveness, you honor yourself as a person, even if you are imperfect. Many people find it difficult to forgive themselves for their actions. Forgive yourself for being in a relationship with the person who hurt you. Or if you were the offender—whether you engaged in extramarital affairs, or substance abuse, or a bad temper, etc. that led to the demise of the relationship, offer an apology to yourself. Your wrongdoing may have caused you to pay tremendous consequences for your actions. Forgiving yourself doesn't absolve you of that responsibility. It forces you to grow, change, and learn. You can still make an all-out effort not to be defined by your past. You can take the actions to heal so that you won't continue to bleed on people who didn't cut you.

The Self-Forgiveness Pledge

Today I choose to forgive myself. I set myself free of the past. I release myself from any offense committed against me or others. I release all of the memories, anger, and hurt about my decisions. My heart is healed. I am whole. My heart is unencumbered. I move forward freely now. I choose to focus on thoughts that strengthen me today— thoughts of peace, love, and harmony.

Doing these exercises and reflections—diving deep into what has hurt you in the past—is what's needed to clear your path to a beautiful relationship. When we've played by the rules and been good women our whole lives, it can seem mysterious why we haven't attracted our Forever Love, but sometimes it's not you as much as that there are blockages. This work will help you heal in places that you may not have consciously considered. It's also a continuous process of discovery when you start forgiveness work. It's something that I still continue to do today in various areas of my life. Think of the hardest thing for you to change and how much you resist it—this is your greatest lesson in your life right now. For many, that lesson is about learning to forgive others and themselves. When we do this, we create space for better relationships.

Move on to what you deserve!

Part IV

JUMPING THE BROOM

Chapter 13

Before the Aisle

"A successful marriage requires falling in love many times, and always with the same person."

—MIGNON MCLAUGHLIN

It's so much fun when the wedding bells are ringing! It's natural for us as humans to cherish companionship, and there's nothing as sweet as when you and The One have found each other and decided to pivot and get that knot tied. He's met and hopefully exceeded your expectations of love. You've found someone who adds happiness to your life (you so deserve it!), and he's everything that makes your heart glow.

Wait, stop. Faith, I'm single, why are we discussing marriage? I'm not there yet!

Because it's important for you to understand the long game even before you're married. I wish a lot of the people who step into my courtroom for a divorce would have. Marriage can be the most amazing, exhilarating relational experience in life. Having a wonderful partner to do life with can be an incredible boost for our well-being.

At the same time, choosing who we marry is a decision with lifelong implications, and it should never be romanticized without acknowledging the real work involved in staying together. Building a strong foundation early on is key. There's a reason fairy tales are called just that: "tales." From books we read as little girls, with a young, impressionable mind, these stories often spark the inception of a lifelong dream that culminates with us believing *Coming to America*'s Prince Hakeem is going to show up and carry us out into the sunset. A happy marriage is not a fairy tale come true; it's a reality you make happen each and every moment.

Marriage is a choice to love, sacrifice, serve, and commit. The Big Day with you in a gorgeous gown, hair and makeup lit, the monster cake, the dance-capade (Kenny and I made a mean dance duo!), and all the applause of your favorite people can be the fantasy part come true, but the reality is what comes after it. Trust me, I deal with the aftermath of marriage every day in court. It's being committed to the same commitment and living life in honor of it. As we've talked about, one of the most important things you can do is build a proper foundation for success. Think about it like this: marriage is the foundation for a home you want to build upon. Do you build on a strong foundation that's been tested to withstand pressure, or do you build on sand? The sturdy foundation is based on your experiences with this person when the two of you are learning about each other. The first thing to know before you even get close to marriage talk is, above all, character matters.

Marcia and Stanley had been married for five years when Marcia appeared before me in *Divorce Court* wanting to officially separate. They'd gotten engaged after knowing each other just three months. When Marcia met Stanley he told her he was a retired Navy SEAL, that he worked for New Jersey governor Chris Christie's security detail, and that he was divorced with one child. His job for the governor, as he told her, was to go out to his apartment balcony and watch Christie's official helicopter land on top of the building next to his and make sure the airspace was clear. She believed him. It was at this moment I contemplated selling her a bridge in Brooklyn! Whew. Everything he told her was a lie. He said he told her those things to impress her. He didn't just not work for Governor Christie—he'd never even met the man! He was still married and actually had nine children—not one! After he got the divorce from the wife he was separated from, Marcia married him. Even after she had discovered he'd fabricated who he was. From the beginning, their entire foundation was based on a lie. The lies didn't change with his new title of "husband." They just got more personal until neither Marcia nor Stanley could parse out truth from fake news. I'd had enough; I released Stanley early from court so he could go on his next fabricated adventure.

My advice to Marcia: The truth may hurt. Lies may sting. But only one sets you free.

Marriage Isn't a Magic Wand

I've had a lot of women come into my courtroom with a laundry list of why they're on the verge of breaking up with their significant other. Everything from cheating, to lying, to controlling behavior. They complain about so many issues with their boyfriends—from he burps too much to his mama is Madea reincarnated—and yet they're still asking for a ring. It's as if a proposal will magically change the bad behavior. It doesn't. If you plan on getting engaged, you best be ready to accept people for who they show themselves to be—whether he's especially flatulent or a mama's boy. Many women make the mistake of marrying for potential. You'll live to regret it. Your entire marriage is based on a hope and prayer the person will change for you. No matter how attractive a person's potential may be, you have to marry their reality. And marriage is no magic wand. The only thing it's guaranteed to change is your legal status. If you need to see change in someone's character in order to be happy in your relationship, it must come before your decision to marry. If your man doesn't know how to treat you before "I do," he'll be just as ignorant afterward. No ring, proposal, or ceremony will change that. A wedding may break the bank, but it won't break bad habits.

If you don't trust your man to go to a party without getting a woman's phone number, how can you trust him to build a life with? When you've invested time, energy, and feelings into a person, a marriage can begin to feel like the next required step and something to cross off a list. So we may force our man to bend like a pretzel instead of acknowledging that a ring will not bring about the change we want. If he isn't good for you now, then he won't be later. I often just want to say: sis, stop trying to promote this man!

And it's not just women who do this! Men too get consumed with the idea that putting a ring on it will make his girlfriend or fiancée into his servant. As if suddenly she'll be making magnificent, elaborate dinners every night and ironing his shirts like his mama did (or never did). I remember one man came into my courtroom who had been dating a traveling nurse. After he proposed, he asked her to quit her job to be a stay-at-home wife or find a job in the city where they were based. She (rightfully) didn't want to quit her job, and they broke up because of that. He couldn't fathom why a woman wouldn't want to be a stay-at-home wife. I had to remind him that there are women who want that, but she wasn't one of them! That's not her fault; he was the one who changed.

So before you go asking for a ring, think long and hard about the person you would be linking yourself to. Being someone's girlfriend and being someone's wife and life partner are two different things. Don't elevate just anyone. When choosing someone to marry, choose somebody who you believe best represents a person 1) who isn't just quick to make promises but is prepared to fulfill those promises, and 2) who takes actions to demonstrate that.

Weddings don't change people—not in the sense of correcting bad behavior. Now, let's talk about the kind of change you should expect to see. Over the years every marriage will go through seasons. You will learn to love the new version of your spouse whom you may not recognize from the day you walked down the aisle. You may have married nineties Brad Pitt but wake up one day to 2021 Brad—same person, different degrees of hotness! You will make a lot of changes whether you want to or not, and so will your spouse. The journey may be filled with peaks and valleys, and you hope to get to the other side gracefully and more in love than ever. But it's not because you married the perfect person or soulmate. That person no longer exists. It's because of your choice to remain committed to the commitment.

You won't be the same person at forty-five that you were at twenty-five. So when people say someone was the perfect person for them but they changed, I always contend there was no such thing. I heard a professor at Duke once say: even if we first marry the right person, just give it a while and he or she will change. Marriage, by virtue of being what it is, means we are not the same person we were when we entered it.

Marriage does change you in these respects—you are constantly negotiating, compromising, and navigating new territory. The primary struggle is learning to love and care for the stranger whom you find yourself married to. There is an illusion that if we find our soulmate all will be magically right in our world. That turns your husband into a god, and no human being can live up to that. He will fall short, and you are setting yourself up for disappointment.

Once we know that there is no person who will magically make everything all right in our world, we can lay the groundwork to make the important decision of who to marry. What is critical to your success? The answer is to do your due diligence—use your discernment to the best of your ability when getting to know them. Then make the best choice you can with the information you have.

There's a funny but powerful *Seinfeld* scene where he is describing marriage as a roller coaster. (Younger people reading may remember this from the intro to Wale's song "Matrimony.") The idea is that no matter what, you can't prepare for the drop. Seinfeld says, "You can't be ready for [marriage] because it's growth, it's gonna be new. You're gonna have a new life, you're gonna be a new person." Instead of spending your entire marriage trying to control everything, work to make sure you're willing to have the flexibility needed to ride the waves of life with another person attached to your life vest. Don't see it as a burden, see it as an opportunity. Many aren't blessed to have a teammate that they can lean on.

Has He Earned a Promotion?

Don't be impressed by money, power, degrees, and looks. I know it's hard; as you can see from my stories, I've gotten caught up by drinking that potion too. Be impressed by generosity, integrity, humility, and kindness—all the things a high-value man represents. At every phase of the relationship's progress you should be asking each other important questions that speak to a person's character, heart, and practical life choices.

When thinking about marriage, have informative discussions to gain an understanding of each other on this topic. Do the two of you see marriage in the same way? Are your visions of marriage in sync? Are the two of you striving for the same thing? The time to get in sync and on the same page is *before* you say "I do." By the time important decision-making is needed, not being on the same page will be lethal for your relationship.

My friend Darius was living in New Orleans with his fiancée years ago. When Hurricane Katrina happened, they were forced to put their wedding on hold and relocate. In the interim, she moved to Detroit for her dream job, and he moved to Charlotte to practice law. They had gone from building a life to long distance, and surprisingly the transition wasn't difficult for them. The challenge came when it was time to pick back up where things left off. A year later it was time to buckle back down and move forward with the wedding. I reached out to congratulate Darius on the coming wedding, and he responded, "Thanks, I guess." Seriously! This wasn't the energy of a man who was confident in the next phase of his life he was stepping into. What had changed?! He didn't want to move to Detroit, and she didn't want to leave her dream job. He figured they'd just work it out, but they never spent the time to get clear on that before the wedding. No surprise to me, they were divorced a year later.

Being smart in love means walking into a marriage with your eyes wide open and a plan in place for your partnership. Revisiting those non-negotiables again is a helpful way of ensuring this is the right step for you two. There are three things that are critical to be on the same page about before you get engaged. Once you embark on a legally binding union, the bar will be raised.

1. **Finances**—I can't stress enough how major finances are to a relationship's success. The majority of the plaintiffs I meet

on *Divorce Court* fell out with their partners over economic stressors. This isn't to say you can't make a relationship work if you have different money habits—you buy all of your shoes from Target and he goes to Gucci—but think long and hard before you walk down the aisle and say those vows, so you can stand on your word. Know who you are marrying and that you're also inheriting financial responsibilities in a marriage. Save the His and Hers for your wardrobes unless you have a prenup. The reality is, if one of you has an immense amount of debt, be absolutely clear on the expectations around that, because that will now become your collective debt. Another common scenario that has led married couples down a messy path is confusion around how expenses would be split. It can get ugly in my courtroom over this—and there's no right or wrong answer. Some people think whoever makes more should pay for more. All I have to say is make sure this is all clear before you put a ring on it. And be prepared to negotiate these terms with love and in a safe environment. I'm always a proponent for surrounding yourself with an expert such as an accountant who you talk to outside of tax season or even a financial advisor. But if that's not your speed, sitting down with just you and your partner to put all the numbers on the table is a great first step. What are your financial goals individually and together? How far are you from them and what's your plan to get there? Don't wait until the bill collectors come calling.

2. **Family**—This is a two-for-one special. Of course, it's important to discuss whether or when to start a family, and hopefully, you've crossed that bridge if you're considering engagement. An area that I see left as an afterthought is the *how* of it all. Are there specific cultural or religious traditions

that are important to you regardless of whether kids are in the picture? Do you have certain ambitions for the trajectory of your life that your partner will need a say in? You two will become a family, not just roommates. It was critical that I find a man who accepted my busy schedule and work ambitions. I'm often traveling, working, or plotting, and I needed someone who could do more than tolerate that but support me in it. Someone who wanted a stay-at-home wife or even someone who was home every night and on the weekends would never be a good fit for me.

What if one of you already has children? Then it's extremely important to navigate the role of a stepparent and what the responsibilities will be. It's a delicate situation when entering a co-parenting relationship, and you should tread both carefully and intentionally. Serve as a sounding board but be cognizant of the part you play. Sit down and answer some questions: How will you ensure quality alone time with the parent and their child? Who will discipline the children and how should that happen? How will the perspective of the other parent be incorporated? What pace will you take when integrating the family?

3. **Communication**—Save "winning" for the lotto. As I've mentioned before, the point of effective communication is not to win but to come to an understanding where both parties can walk away feeling heard and understood. And what all of this truly boils down to is, are you talking *to and with* each other or *at* each other? A lot will change after you say "I do," both in the world around you and within you. So it's no wonder that arguments, disagreements, or challenges will rise up, but communication is what quells them. Communication shows that you are both committed to hearing each

other and that you trust each other enough to never make assumptions without checking in. Whether it's grudges, silent treatment, or other toxic practices, remove them from your arsenal and let talking be your go-to. I assure you it will save you time and time again.

Before you proceed to choosing marriage, it helps first to understand what partnership will ultimately boil down to. It looks like choosing someone who you will have 10,000-plus meals with. Have 50,000-plus conversations with. You will hear about their day 100,000-plus times. If you choose to have children, they will greatly influence your legacy. It's one of the most important choices you'll make in life. Please don't make this choice half-heartedly.

There are pros and cons. The positive side is you have someone on this journey of life. Someone to hug. Someone to eat the other half of the Family Size Doritos if you buy it. A lot of people like to look at this as: you're not alone. It's beautiful to have a sounding board for your ideas, a shoulder to lean on, and a companion for your Netflix binges. The trade-off is you're *never* alone! All of the decisions you used to make about life, career, finances, home are now made with another person in mind. You give up certain freedom and liberties and compromise tremendously as a part of being a "we"—a team versus an "I." When you choose to partner, you must make room in every aspect of your life for another human being.

The Relationship Board of Directors

I was once dating a man who, like me, worked in the public eye. I made a decision early on that we should keep our relationship private, save a few close friends and family, but it soon became clear that we weren't on the same page. He resented my decision and felt my refusal to make our relationship public was indicative of him not being good enough. I wish I had seen that for the red flag it was, but we continued having the same discussion over and over (about that and other issues) until I eventually ended the relationship. I thought our story would end there, but unfortunately it didn't.

A few weeks later, a mutual friend of ours told me she'd heard him on an Instagram live chat where he not only allowed someone to name-drop me but said *I* was the insecure one. We had agreed not to go public when we were dating, but now that I'd ended it, he thought it was a way to get back at me. I felt blindsided by the betrayal and embarrassed at the messiness of it all. By this time, I had grown as a person and wasn't the least bit interested in his vengeful game. It wasn't my personality to say insulting things in public about anyone, and especially not someone who I'd once felt so close to. So I said nothing and left it to a higher power to resolve. And do you know what that got me that the apartment shakedown didn't? Peace. **Pro tip:** avoid people who badmouth their exes on social media or public forums. It's a red flag signifying they don't know how to manage their anger or hurt in an emotionally mature way. If not addressed, it will continue to manifest itself in every relationship they have, including the one with you. In other words, if things don't work out, he *will* try to put you on blast, sis. *Run.*

From the very beginnings of our relationships we are often advised to keep our personal affairs private—not just with the general public but with most folks—and for good reason! "Keep people out of your business!" is what we're often told. Why?

Because not everyone's advice is solid. And a public gaze is especially just too many cooks in the kitchen for me. That would burn the whole relationship down. The same thing goes with our beloved friends and family who love us so much. Instead of feeding the fire to them with every little fight, disagreement, or struggle that you and the other half have, opt to operate like a team and maintain a certain level of privacy that protects your trust in each other. When we vent about our partners to friends and family, we open up the chance that grudges could get held or divides be created where there should be unity. It's not keeping your loved ones out of the marriage or relationship, it's protecting them from it.

You should have confidants who give you advice and offer wisdom—but choose wisely. Kenny and I had a well-formed Relationship Board of Directors before we got married. We were not playing games. I repeat, we were not playing games.

When you transition from being a couple in a relationship to a married couple, it's nearly impossible to do so alone. With any major milestone, we surround ourselves with good counsel. When launching a business, we assemble a board of advisors to steer toward professional success. When having a baby, we appoint godparents in case of an emergency to ensure the child's care and protection. Marriage is no different! Break the stigma of not seeking support in your relationship. There's no shame in seeking counseling, and it's not an indicator of conflict!

Before we were married, Kenny and I surrounded ourselves with a community of people who were committed to our success. For me it boils down to what we talked about in chapter 3 about ego. There's no space in a relationship for being too proud to ask for help. The smartest people don't know it all, but they know when and how to draw on the strengths of others. The fact that you're reading this book is proof enough that you value the expertise of others and care enough about love to invest. Go deeper when you've found Mr. Right by identifying people who can be a sounding board about how to continue building on a strong foundation.

This doesn't mean listen to any and everybody—remember

Auntie or Cousin So-and-So was always a mess and you don't need her in your business. I never listen to criticism from people I wouldn't take advice from. But for those who you do trust, turn them into your secret weapon, employ them as your Relationship's Board of Directors: people you can count on for helpful perspective, sound advice, and insight based on their own experiences and track records.

Kenny and I made it our mission to surround ourselves with those whose advice we collectively valued, and it made all the difference. Sure, it's helpful to have a girlfriend who is loyal to you alone, but that's who you go to for your personal empowerment. Friends who know and love you both as individuals and as a pair are who you turn to for meaningful advice. For us, those people included Aaron Lindsey, the pastor and music producer who introduced us; Brian Holland, the pastor who did our pre-engagement counseling; and the pastor who performed our marriage ceremony, DeVon Franklin.

When I met Aaron, he had been married for twenty-two years to his wife, Adrian. I witnessed their happy and healthy union from afar until I got to know them personally. It shined through even more. I could talk for days about the impact Aaron had on our union, but I'll save some of that for the next chapter. DeVon's candor made him the perfect resource. He reminded us that what we share is ordained by God and that leaning on Him keeps our eyes on the prize. DeVon was *such* a blessing to Kenny and me when we were considering marriage that we asked him to officiate at our wedding and set the stage for our union.

Take a few minutes to think of the people in your life who can be your Aaron or DeVon. Someone with a relationship that most *feels* like the one you are aspiring to. I say "feel" instead of "look" for a reason—don't settle on those with the most beautifully pack-aged relationship. Find the people in your life who communicate clearly and consistently, who know how to listen, and who are not impulsive.

Sometimes you may want to pull in the support of someone from outside of your network for confidentiality and a fresh outlook. This was the case for Kenny and me. We were attending a friend's wedding, and the officiating pastor was dropping amazing gems, not just for the couple but for all of us present. That's how we met Pastor Brian Holland.

On the flip side of all of this, you should not take advice from strangers on the internet! As I mentioned, I had to halt my ex putting our business on the internet for my own mental peace. I've seen couples air their dirty laundry online only to find that when they work things out with their significant other, they now have to worry about naysayers and their unsolicited opinions about whether they did the right thing or not.

Lucy came into *Divorce Court* with Damien, whom she'd been married to for five years. She told me that whenever she wanted an opinion about what was going on with their marriage, she would go on Facebook and pose "general questions." I told Lucy navigating marriage is already difficult enough with having to balance time, space, and privacy. Why would she take it to the internet streets to ask people she doesn't know to give their opinion about a relationship they don't care about? Make it make sense, Lucy! Don't invite any and everyone into your relationship. Marriage is sacred; treat it so.

Pay Now or Pay Later

Let's call a thing a thing: pre-engagement counseling is just what it sounds like, counseling before engagement. Somehow there's a big ole ugly stigma about couples therapy, but why? I don't understand why this is considered bad or weird, especially for those who aren't married yet. Many people hear "therapy" and think there must be something wrong. I approach the health of a relationship the way I do anything else: preventative is key. Why wait for the wheels to fall off when you can maintain it over time and avoid the breakdown altogether?

The only relationship in which I actually went through with counseling was with my current husband. (Go figure!) Initially I was nervous to bring it up to Kenny, precisely because I know how stigmatized therapy or counseling is, especially for Black men. We had never even argued, and I worried he'd bristle at the first mention of counseling to dive deeper. For me, therapy isn't an indictment but rather a reflection of just how much I valued who we were becoming together. I didn't want anything—big or small—to jeopardize us, and I thought pre-engagement counseling would make sure of that.

Luckily for me, Kenny couldn't have agreed more. Not only did he not run away in fear, but his first response was to recommend the pastor we had seen at the wedding. There were so many moments in our relationship when I knew Kenny was an amazing man, but this was one that topped the list. He cared as much about our future as I did, and he wasn't afraid to not just show up, but show some initiative as well.

Everyone wants to be Michael Jordan, but no one wants to put the time in at the gym. The same goes for love! Everyone wants the bae-cations, yet few are willing to show up on the hard days. This isn't to say that therapy has to be difficult, but, inherently, there will be some discomfort in being so vulnerable. In those sessions, we had no one but each other and our pastor. There was no audience to fake it for, and we were able to have important conversations about our values, expectations, and desires.

Our pastor asked us questions I don't know if I would have thought to ask otherwise. And more than that, he gave us materials to read together so that our work wouldn't end when we left his office. The exercises and materials he took us through confirmed what we knew: that we were ready. It encouraged us to have the blessing of someone we trusted and who flat out told us that if we needed more time he wouldn't hold back. Our pastor ended up being one of the speakers at our wedding.

The conversations we had together prior to any rings made saying "I do" even easier. We had no cold feet, no trepidation, no uncertainty. No one ever knows all the things life will throw at them (like being married for one week before being quarantined for months in a pandemic!), but I did know that I trusted my husband, and I learned how much our backgrounds had shaped our perspectives. There's no doubt that whatever comes our way, we're equipped to take it on headfirst. Knowing that we are truly a united force made becoming Mrs. Lattimore a joy rather than a fear. Take the time and go long before you accept a ring. Announce your desire to marry this person to yourself first, and take the steps to build a solid foundation.

Of all the couples I've met in *Divorce Court*—I've never had one tell me they wished they'd moved faster to get married. They all say they wish they'd taken more time. When you're coupled and thinking about taking the big leap, here are ten questions to ask:

10 Questions Before the Aisle

1. What examples of love and marriage shape your expectations for our union?

2. What's something you've had to forgive someone for? How did you go about doing that?

3. What is the worst thing a lover/partner could do, in your eyes?

4. Everyone has a breaking point. What is considered a deal-breaker action to you?

5. What's one thing you've always wanted to say to me but never have?

6. What are some traditions or practices that you don't do now but that feel important for you to do with your future family/children? (Like religion or holidays.)

7. What is the biggest lesson life has taught you, and how has it changed your behavior or actions?

8. When we disagree on important decisions, how do you think we should break the tie?

9. How much debt do you have, and what's your plan for paying it off?

10. If you could fast-forward twenty years, what do you envision for your life?

The secret to happiness in marriage revolves around one simple factor: how you treat each other. When kindness, service, diplomacy, and respect are the foundation, it's a space where love can thrive.

The years and lifetime spent together can often change the nature of how we treat our significant others. But if there's one person on the face of the Earth you should show kindness and respect to, it should be the person to whom you're married. That person before anyone else. And yet in all too many homes, that's the last person to be treated that way.

While writing this book, I recently celebrated my first wedding anniversary. In addition to my own experience, I've spent time with many, *many* couples in my profession. I've learned that it takes practice and work to be thoughtful every day to the person you're married to, and that's exactly what makes a marriage work—working to continue to show up kind, loving, and thoughtful. People often think there is some kind of mystery to a really great and successful marriage. Trust me, there's not. I've seen disasters in sickness and in health, till side chicks do us part. Therefore all have the ability to succeed or not. There's no mystery. Everything operates on the same law of cause and effect. The yard around your house will reflect exactly the care you are giving it. It can return to you only the beauty and abundance that you're willing to put into it. If you don't pull the weeds, water it, mow it, and prune it, it grows out of control and will descend into chaos.

It's the same with a job, a business, a human life, a marriage—with everything.

You can tell exactly what people are putting into a marriage by observing what the marriage is returning to them. The most important ingredient is how you choose to treat the other and show love. How do you feel toward anyone who treats you with kindness and respect? You like that person, and you like to be around them. Well, the same common sense and principles are applied to the one person on Earth you've decided to spend your life with. When applied, they take on a whole world of new meaning and build a foundation of solid rock and the love you found for each other.

This is why we call it Forever Love.

Chapter 14

Ain't Nothing Like the Real Thing, Baby

"The real act of marriage takes place in the heart, not in the ball-room or church or synagogue."

—BARBARA DE ANGELIS

If you want "Happily Ever After," then you have to bring the *happy* to your *ever after*. Otherwise, the notion of happily ever after is unrealistic and creates harmful ideas of what partnership and marriage are truly about. But just because I'm a realist about love doesn't mean I'm not a romantic. In fact, I'm head over heels in and about love precisely because true love, *real* love, is way better than the movies. It's unexpected and fills you up in every way imaginable. I've shared bits and pieces of Kenny's and my story throughout the book, but I want to paint the picture for you of what brought us together.

In 2019 I was going through a transition period. I'd just got out of a relationship (yes, another one—listen, I was in these dating streets for a while). It was an amicable but painful ending. And my TV show *Judge Faith* had already ended, so for the first time in my career I wasn't working. I was in a period of unknowing as my romantic and professional lives were in limbo. I was at a crossroads, and I had to make a choice how to move forward.

When I realized I wasn't going to see the person I had been dating anymore, I gave myself time for a good cathartic cry. About an hour later, I decided it was time to dry my tears and apply everything I'd learned about radical acceptance and what it meant to let go in peace. I realized that I had an opportunity here: plenty of free time to invest in myself so that when my work and love lives picked back up, I'd be ready for the next level. I also made a decision when the relationship ended that this would be my last breakup. I had an honest, transparent conversation with God. I said, *God, you've seen my journey. I've learned a lot over the years while dating and it's during this time in my life when I'm yet hurting again that I'm going to show you. Despite how I feel, I believe this is all working out for my good. I release this relationship and this person and I accept the man you have for me, my husband. I will pass this test in my life and believe that this ending is opening the door for a new beginning with the man I will marry.* I then took out a sheet of paper on my birthday and wrote, "By this time next year I'll be engaged to _____." Then I controlled the biggest battle of them all: the one in my mind. I would only think thoughts that aligned with my prayer—that aligned with what I wrote. I went to bed at night visualizing my dream manifesting. I told my two closest friends that I would be meeting my husband in the coming year. And not only would he meet my expectations, he would exceed them. I knew beyond a shadow of a doubt my time had come! Some of you may be thinking with all the stories I've shared: I sure hope so! While I believed in the manifestation for my life, I also went on living.

I started by staying off of social media for a while for my own mental health. I didn't want to fill the space in my life with hot air

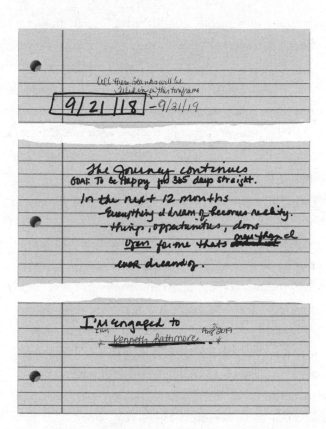

and a need for external validation. I wanted to do all I could do to show myself love and embrace my solitude to see what fruit that tree would bear. During that time I decided to pick back up singing. Back in my pageant days, singing was my talent and also my escape. Music had always brought me deep joy, and so I decided to rekindle that flame.

Like any aspect of my life, I pursued music with a hunger. I started taking vocal lessons and then went a step further—I decided to try my hand at recording a Christmas single! Something fun, but also out of my comfort zone to scratch my itch and try to do something new. As I said, I wasn't interested in doing anything halfway, so I reached out to someone considered a "super producer" or hit-maker whom I had worked with in the past. I wanted to see what the process of putting out a single would look like from one of the best in the game. Aaron Lindsey, the Grammy-winning music producer I mentioned before, had worked with some of the biggest stars in the business, so I didn't expect that he'd work with me. But I figured he would at least take my call and I could get some insight, and maybe even a referral.

When he responded saying that he was open to talking, I was thrilled! We met up in person over coffee, and I was just soaking up the knowledge, taking notes in my planner, and asking tons of follow-up questions. I had no ulterior motive but bettering myself, and yet the producer took note. At the end of our meeting, he asked if I was married. I was a bit surprised at the question, but of course I responded honestly that I wasn't. He then asked me what I was look-ing for in a husband, and after I shared some obligatory things he said he'd keep an eye out. I thought nothing further of it.

At this point in my life I knew that my past relationships had not worked out for a reason. I knew that, one day, I would meet that *reason*. Have a conversation with that *reason*. Fall in love with that *reason*. And shortly after that initial conversation with Aaron, he indeed introduced me to my *reason*. Unbeknownst to me, after that meeting he went home and spoke to his wife about setting me up with their friend of fifteen years—R & B legend Kenny Lattimore.

Now, as you might imagine, I'd been through my share of blind dates. And I wasn't new to people thinking they knew the "perfect person" for me, so before I knew who the setup would be with, I was questioning whether to accept. I had a flashback to my cousin Freda (yes, the one with the dry dressing)—she was always trying to set the women in the family up with folks from her church. Let my cousin Freda tell it, Little Union Baptist Church had the hottest bachelors in town. She once set me up with a guy named Caron—one of the church deacon's grandsons. Caron and I went to the state fair on a first date. I watched him scarf down three corn dogs and four beers then get into an altercation with a fair worker, accusing him of cheating at miniature free-throw basketball. The funny part was all of this was over him trying to win me an overstuffed teddy bear. I was so embarrassed that I channeled my inner Keke Palmer and told security: "I don't know this man…" We were escorted out of the fair by flashlight security, and I've never let her set any of us up with anyone ever since!

Back to Aaron: He was hesitant because he didn't want to overstep his professional boundaries too far with me, but his wife asked him: "What does your heart tell you?" He said: "It's telling me that they are perfect for each other." In a world of swiping right and blind dates, I was grateful to meet Kenny through someone who could vouch for him. I vividly remember Aaron telling me, "He's an amazing singer but an even better person. He has a beautiful spirit." My goodness, he was right. And just like that—in the pursuit of doing something I loved—I ultimately met my Forever Love.

When I was first told about Kenny, I didn't automatically think, "That's my husband!" I knew my prayer, but I also knew I had to do my part, which was to make prudent decisions. Here he was walking into the room to meet me—his clothes fit him perfectly, his smile brightened the entire room, but I thought, *Do we have enough in common?* Everyone thought I was gonna marry a Harvard-educated attorney and be one half of that kind of power couple. There was a specific ex that I dated back in New York, Damon, who fit that bill and was working at a top global firm. We were a great-looking couple and everything worked on paper.

But in real life, this man could *not* keep a job! It was all smoke and mirrors—and not just for his career. He turned out to be just as inconsistent in his relationships as he was with his work. I never envisioned myself dating an R & B singer mainly because it wasn't the world I was in, so professionally Kenny would not be the type of man in my inner circle. Then the idea of dating a performer who was so widely beloved, on the road touring and performing, and with a fan base that consisted 80 percent of women wasn't really the life I envisioned. Admittedly, I had some stereotypical views.

But in one two-hour conversation over lunch, all that came to a head. I knew he was something special. And when I got the chance to intimately know his spirit and get to know him as a person, not just what he does for a living, everything changed. He was kind, humble, smart, genuine, and giving. He'd been in the music business for twenty-five years, so he'd crossed a lot of paths. And everywhere I went, I found out that everywhere he'd gone he'd left a path of people who loved him. Unbeknownst to me, a good friend of mine had actually worked with him on a project—and when he found out that we had met, he told me that he has always been such a nice, stand-up person. Another wall in my heart came down.

Early on, it was clear that we had way more in common than we might have thought. I connected with him more than I ever did with the Harvard litigator. It was deeper than more superficial things and directed more toward our shared outlooks on life. The time we spent together on early dates dispelled any ideas I had about whether we could work. There was a calmness that washed over us, and I felt a peace I'd never felt before. It was also ironic that I had spent so much time becoming a boss babe in my eyes, and here I was dating the man I'd marry—and for the first time in my life I didn't have a job. I was developing projects and going to meetings, but nothing had panned out yet. So when Kenny and I got to know each other, I wasn't under the glitz and glamour of TV or rushing off to cover some high-profile case—in some ways it left me feeling vulnerable about how he would perceive my career. In other ways I realized that my work didn't have to define who I was. I became fully present.

In addition to our dates, we spent hours on the phone talking about everything from our faith to our shared interest in books. We talked about our hobbies, good food, and biggest fears. I learned that before any record deal, he had attended the illustrious Howard University for architecture. He got to hear about my Wall Street days. By the time we got to our fourth date, I think we both knew we'd found someone special in each other. As time went on, we also knew we had some differences—Kenny was far more organized and structured. His home looked like a model home; meanwhile, due to my schedule-juggling nature, I am way more grab-and-go. Our differences aren't character flaws, they just make us who we are. Still, we knew we wanted to dig deeper before embarking on a lifetime commitment.

One night Kenny and I went out to dinner with Aaron and his wife, Adrian. During dinner as the guys were talking, Adrian leaned over and told me that they had been praying for Kenny to meet someone amazing because he deserved it. Then with the next words out of her mouth, I felt my heart open in a way I'd never experienced. She said, when a woman meets a person with Kenny's heart, spirit, and talent they might start looking for flaws—waiting for the other shoe to drop. She continued, "But you can rest. There is no other shoe. This is who he really is." And in that moment, I exhaled. It's like an angel had been sent to give me that message. All the tears, all the past pain, all the hurt, all the work to overcome it all—here I was sitting next to the man I knew I would marry. He would indeed get the best version of me. And I of him. He too had been through breakups, hurt, and even a divorce. But what I admired about Kenny the most was that he didn't allow any pain from his past to harden his heart. He walked through those challenging times with integrity, refusing to publicly respond to statements meant to embarrass or belittle him. Instead of rushing in to vindicate himself, he took away its only power: his attention. He was a high-value man operating in high-value ways. In addition, he knew going negative would hurt his child. He was acutely aware of how children look to their parents the most for guidance on how to model love, especially in the midst of challenging times. I've found that he lives his entire life in this manner—choosing to believe what the scripture actually says: the weapons formed against you simply can't prosper. In the end, I felt like our love was a part of his reward.

On a cool September afternoon in Central Park in the city where my love journey had started some fifteen years earlier, I turned around after having a brief conversation with a stranger who had walked over to talk to Kenny, and I saw that Kenny was getting down on one knee. The stranger—a man I'd never seen before in my life—then reached in his pocket and pulled out a small box. He placed the box in Kenny's hand, and that's when I knew what was happening and the tears started rolling down my face. I remembered the moment in college in that car when the Brian McKnight song (the irony!) played and I had looked up at the stars to think about my ex. I thought about all of the lessons I'd learned in dating and relationships and my resolve to never settle. Now, here I was in the moment that I had envisioned, with a man who was better than I could have imagined down on one knee proposing to me. The stranger was indeed one of Kenny's childhood friends he'd flown in from Oklahoma to hold the ring and help him procure the perfect surprise proposal. It was beautiful and perfect. There was no hesitation, and the easiest decision I ever made when I said YES! Eleven months after I wrote that I would meet my husband in the next year, I officially became engaged.

The end, right?! Happily ever after? Well, 2020 had something to say about that!

Kenny and I were married on March 8, 2020. It was a beautiful ceremony with close to 300 of our friends and family in attendance. Stevie Wonder (humble brag!) sang as I walked down the aisle, and there wasn't a dry eye in the church. A lot more tears would have been shed if we had known what was really about to happen in the world! Less than a week later, half the country would be limiting travel and locking down public places in response to the COVID-19 outbreak. By the end of the month, the entire world was on lockdown, and we had no idea when that would change. We had had just enough time to formalize our partnership, but we were still in our infancy when we realized we'd be spending much of our newlywed time quarantined with each other in Los Angeles. While it wasn't at all what we had planned for the year, the time together ended up being a huge blessing to our relationship. A time that represented new challenges for everyone had also granted us a priceless resource: quality time.

Kenny and I weren't alone in being coupled in isolation. This is where our vows got tested. Unfortunately, I know many couples who only survive with the help of buffers and crutches. Whether through working a lot, being too busy for each other, or escaping to other friends and loved ones, many were unprepared for the extended period of time without the noise. For us, the time was glorious! Quarantine was like noise-cancelling headphones, and while we pivoted in our careers and kept busy enough, we also got to be each other's priority. We used the time to our advantage and built our foundation in ways that can take some couples years.

What I knew before we got married is that Kenny's mood isn't influenced by what happens in his day. His positivity has always been infectious. With our schedules shut down, I got to truly relish that. He always wakes up in a good mood, exuding happiness, which has helped me intentionally start my day in the same manner. The best of him rubbed off on me and vice versa.

We also learned how to be still. Before the quarantine, we would pride ourselves on being on the go. Hustling. Grinding. Pursuing the next big goal. In fact, we had taken time and done our annual vision boards together on January 1 (the pandemic was not a part of our plans!); 2020 became the year that we may not have gotten everything we wanted on those boards, but it was the year we truly appreciated everything we had.

Chapter 15

It's in Your Hands

"The most common way people give up their power is thinking they don't have any."

—ALICE WALKER

Let me tell you an old proverb that is always so timely for me! There was a wise woman who once lived by herself near a small village. Rumor had it that she could always accurately predict when the rains would come, or help heal a sick child with herbs, or help angry neighbors resolve their disputes. People came from all over the land to meet with her and seek advice. Her reputation was such that it was said she was never wrong—not ever.

Some of the children of the village didn't believe that it was possible to always be right. Surely she could not know everything! They decided to test her knowledge. First they asked her to answer questions about the planets, the animals, and the world. No matter how hard the questions, she always answered correctly.

The children were amazed at her knowledge and learning, and most were ready to stop testing the wise woman. However, one boy was determined to prove that the old woman couldn't know everything. He told all of his friends to meet him at the woman's home the following afternoon so he could prove she was a fake.

The next day he caught a bird. Holding it behind his back so no one could see what was in his hands, he walked triumphantly to the wise woman's home.

"Old woman!" he called. "Come and show us how wise you are!"

The woman walked calmly to the door. "May I help you?" she simply asked.

"You say you know everything. Prove it—what am I holding behind my back?" the young boy demanded.

The woman thought for a moment. She could make out the faint sounds of a bird's wings rustling. "I do not say I know everything—for that would be impossible," she replied. "However, I do believe you are holding a bird in your hands."

The boy was furious. How could the woman have possibly known he had a bird? Thinking quickly, he came up with a new scheme. He would ask the woman whether the bird was alive or dead. If the woman replied, "Alive," he would crush it with his hands and prove her wrong. If she answered, "Dead," on the other hand, he would pull the living bird from behind his back and allow it to fly away. Either way, he would prove his point, and the wise woman would be discredited.

"Very good," he called. "It is a bird. But tell me, is the bird I am holding alive or dead?"

The wise woman paused for a long moment while the boy waited with anticipation for his opportunity to prove her wrong. Again the woman spoke calmly. "The answer, my young friend, is in your hands."

The boy realized that the wise woman had once again spoken correctly and truthfully. The answer was indeed in his own hands. Feeling the bird feebly moving in his hands as it tried to escape his grasp, he felt suddenly very ashamed and walked away, setting the bird free.

I love that story, and I enjoy telling it because it's a reminder that we hold in our hands the keys to our future. The old woman wasn't reading minds or seeing into the future; she was wise enough to use her full senses and let people do with that information what they would. The real secret to attracting a true partner is not just luck or random coincidences—it's in your hands.

It's in your hands.

Remember, you get to choose the woman you want to be. You get to discard the thoughts and habits that aren't serving you, and create new ones that do. Align your actions with that highest, most exquisite vision of yourself, and watch your entire life change.

The key to your happiness should never be in the hands of another person.

Your hands are a symbol for your consciousness. You are guided by your inner being that wants, above all else, peace.

Set Intention

Write down what it is you want in your love life going forward. Put it up where you can see it every day for the next thirty days. Read it every morning when you wake up and every night before you go to bed. What you focus on is exactly the direction you'll see your life go. Refuse to think negative, defeating thoughts that limit you.

Here's what I wrote (and read daily) the year before I met my husband:

> I am in a divine relationship that's leading to engagement and marriage.

I am fearless, unafraid, and confident as all my dreams manifest. I have a cheerful and positive outlook and demeanor about life.

Forever Love does *not* just happen. The space for it has to be created within and beyond you. When I moved to New York and didn't know a single soul, I wanted to make friends. Well, I couldn't do that by sitting alone in my apartment every chance I got and being a snob to people I met. I had to be intentional about it. I became purposeful about making that wish a reality. I was proactive about planning girls' nights and being present for their important milestones. It wasn't enough to wish and hope good friends would appear. It all started with one thing: a decision.

As my grandma Ella Mae used to tell me: *Faith without works is dead*. You can't passively wait for dreams to come to you. You must move toward them. You can't spend your life reacting to everything that happens around you and waiting for the magic to happen for the life you want. You must make conscious choices that reflect the desired outcome you seek. Open your heart at every moment to the partnership you seek to attract—and do the work necessary as we've outlined in this book to make that partnership happen.

Conclusion

A Promise

I know what it's like to be looked at as a woman achieving in every area of life—except love. The funny thing is, you're always achieving when you're growing and learning. I went to the school of hard knocks. I learned by trial and error, sometimes trial by fire.

But I learned the absolute truth about love: you can manifest the love of your dreams. Some of the best advice I was ever given when I took my first job out of school was "You will win if you don't quit." I've seen this come true in my life time and again. When you stand in the truth of who you are and what you believe, even in the face of the world telling you otherwise, and you refuse to quit, you will win.

I promise you, you don't need to settle in our homes, careers, intellectually—and you definitely don't need to settle in a relationship. I've written *Sis, Don't Settle* to enforce in women that living a purposeful life needs to be the priority. I've listed a whole load of mistakes that I made and other women I know have made because we were settling. This is the book that I wish I had sooner. It would have saved me a lot of tears, time, and even money.

I found my person, as Shonda Rhimes coined it in *Grey's Anatomy*. The person I will spend forever with. Whom I can talk to for hours on end without running out of something to say. Who lights up my world with his smile and melts my heart with his voice. Who is my biggest cheerleader and pushes me to be my brightest, best self. The person whom I agree to disagree with, hide the retail delivery boxes from, but never eat the last cookie. I wish that for each of you. I firmly believe that if you follow the principles in this book, you will achieve the genuine love you desire. And I hope that when you find this love, you appreciate it so deeply that you never lose sight of its goodness. You deserve that and more.

Acknowledgments

Throughout my journey in life there have been many people who have encouraged, supported, and inspired me all along the way. Their love lifts me higher every day.

To my husband, Kenny, you are a dream come true, and your support for me while writing this book made it all possible. Your prayers, grace, patience, and covering are an immense blessing in my life. You are a rare soul in this world, and your beautiful voice pales in comparison to the beauty of your spirit.

To my family—my mom, siblings, nieces, and nephews, who are always there to cheer me on, you all inspire me to keep pushing and dream bigger.

To my dad, who is watching all of this from a better place, I realize how much my sense of humor comes from you. Thank you for blessing me with the ability to laugh and see the lighter side of all things.

To my literary agent, Brandi Bowles, who encouraged me to write this book and believed in its potential even before I saw it, thank you for pushing me in the right direction.

Thank you to my brilliant editor, Krishan Trotman—I learned so much from you during this process. You are creating a legacy of brilliant writers and work for years to come.

Brea Baker—thank you for your incredible mind and skill set in helping bring this book and these words to life!

I would also like to acknowledge the amazing viewers of the longest-running daytime court show on TV: *Divorce Court*. You all are so engaging about the relationships we feature, and your perspectives are always so insightful. To every person who has ever appeared before me in court and shared your story, I hope you left with your load a little lighter.

Thank you to the good Lord from which all blessings flow. I am immensely blessed by the grace bestowed upon my life.

Notes

Carina Hsieh and Taylor Andrews, "Just a Bunch of Questions to Ask When You Really Want to Get to Know Someone," Cosmo politan.com, April 14, 2021. https://www.cosmopolitan.com /sex-love/a29774929/questions-to-get-to-know-someone/.

Chérie Carter-Scott, *If Love Is a Game, These Are the Rules* (London: Ebury Digital, 2010), Kindle.

Leena Lomeli, "Your Relationships Are Only as Healthy as You," Thought Catalog, December 19, 2017. https://thoughtcatalog .com/leena-lomeli/2017/12/your-relationships-are-only-as -healthy-as-you/.

Andy Stanley, *The New Rules for Love, Sex, and Dating* (Grand Rap- ids, MI: Zondervan, 2015).